DIVINE
INTUITION

3 0012 00249347 5

D0716331

ROM STOCK

DRAWN FROM STOCK

DIVINE INTUITION

Lynn A. Robinson, M.Ed.

Foreword by Cheryl Richardson
Author of *Take Time for Your Life*

LIMERICK COUNTY LIBRARY

HU37 3u

153
44

A DORLING KINDERSLEY BOOK

Dorling  Kindersley

LONDON, NEW YORK, SYDNEY, DELHI, PARIS,
MUNICH, and JOHANNESBURG

Editorial director LaVONNE CARLSON
Art director TINA VAUGHAN
Managing editor GILLIAN ROBERTS
Managing art editor TRACEY WARD
Project editor BARBARA MINTON
Art direction MASON LINKLATER
Production ELIZABETH CHERRY, MARYANN ROGERS
JOANNA BULL

First published in Great Britain in 2001 by
Dorling Kindersley Limited
9 Henrietta Street, London WC2E 8PS

Copyright © 2001 Dorling Kindersley Publishing, Inc.
Text copyright © 2001 Lynn A. Robinson
Foreword copyright © 2001 Cheryl Richardson

All rights reserved. No part of this publication may be
reproduced, stored in a retrieval system, or transmitted, in any
form or by any means, electronic, mechanical, photocopying,
recording, or otherwise without the prior written permission
of the copyright owners.

A CIP catalogue record for this book is available from
The British Library

ISBN 0 7513 0858 7

Text film out by Creative Text & Graphical Innovations Ltd
Reproduced in Singapore by Colourscan
Printed and bound by L. Rex Printing Company Limited, China

See our complete catalogue at

www.dk.com

CONTENTS

FOREWORD

by Cheryl Richardson, author of TAKE TIME FOR YOUR LIFE

FROM THE AGE OF THIRTEEN I HAD A DREAM TO PUBLISH A BOOK. YEAR AFTER YEAR, AS I WROTE IN MY JOURNAL, I fantasized about living the life of an author. Twenty-five years later, I finally got my chance.

When my work as a personal coach was featured in a national magazine, and a publisher expressed interest, I began the hard work of putting together a book proposal. For more than six months I dedicated each day to crafting my book, committed to getting it just right. On the day that I finished, I realized that I had no idea what to do next. Should I send it off to a publisher, find an agent, or hire a writer to check my grammar?

What I did know however, was how to use my intuition to ask for the guidance that I needed in order to take the next step. Throughout the previous ten years, I had gradually learned to stop, check in, connect with my inner wisdom, and act.

So here I was standing in the middle of my office when I decided to ask for divine guidance. "OK, God," I said, "If I'm meant to publish a book, I need directions on what to do next. And," I continued, "I need them right now." Immediately a woman's name popped into my head. She was someone from my past that had been involved in the publishing field. Knowing that it was important to act on whatever guidance I received, I immediately picked up the phone and called Maggie. "Maggie," I said, "I just finished writing my first book proposal and I have no idea what to do next. I stopped to ask God for direction and your name popped into my head. I wondered if you have any ideas?"

"That's funny," Maggie said, "yesterday, I had lunch with an editor who just left her job at a major publishing house to do freelance editing. During lunch, she happened to mention the article about you and expressed an interest in your work. You might want to have her take a look at your proposal before you send it anywhere. Why don't you give her a call?"

When Maggie gave me this helpful information I was not surprised by the synchronicity of this event. I'd experienced the power of intuition in my life many times before. These are the kinds of "magical coincidences" that occur when you learn how to ask for and act on the intuitive information you receive. Learning about the practical ways that you can tap into your Divine Intuition is what this book is all about.

I've had the pleasure of knowing Lynn Robinson for more than fifteen years and I must say there are few people more qualified than her to teach others about accessing and using the power of Divine Intuition. In this book, she does what so few teachers do: She combines spiritual wisdom with practical advice to help you discover your best path to a life that you love. Lynn and I met at a holistic education center in Watertown, Massachusetts, called The Interface Foundation. As one of the most popular teachers, Lynn's two programs: "Creating the Life You Want" and "Developing Your Intuition" were always filled to capacity. Lynn was smart. She focused her teaching on the practical ways that her students could make intuition a part of their everyday lives. Her approachable style and commitment to live by the guiding principles she spoke about make her a gifted teacher and wise friend.

There are many paths to creating a life you love. No path is better or worse. What's wonderful about this book is that it will guide you to the most important path of all – the path that's right for you. When you learn to develop and trust your Divine Intuition, you begin to live an authentic, meaningful life – the kind of life you were meant to live.

By the way, when I followed my Divine Intuition and called the woman that Maggie recommended, she not only agreed to review my proposal, she became the guardian angel who helped bring my life's dream to fruition. Don't wait to fulfill your dreams and create a life you love; start now by reading and applying the valuable principles that Lynn Robinson has to offer.

Cheryl Richardson

INTRODUCTION

I believe in intuition. I believe in living my life intuitively.

DREAMS ARE A VITAL SOURCE FOR INTUITIVE INFORMATION. My technique for accessing guidance from dreams is to write a few paragraphs about a current problem or concern before I go to bed at night. I then try to summarize my concern into a question. I imagine that I am releasing this question to a being or power I experience as God. I fully expect an answer. It may not come by morning but it always arrives. Sometimes I receive an answer that comes into my thoughts fully formed. Many times I receive a little fragment of information, a whisper from my soul.

Here is a sample paragraph I wrote before going to bed in September of 1997: I have been praying for some months now about my next steps, my life purpose. I have a successful business giving intuitive readings to individuals from all walks of life. They call me from all over the world. I feel richly blessed. I have an abundance of clients. I love what I do. I feel guilty that I'm not satisfied with the rich abundance I have in my work. I feel I am of service to the people I speak with as well as to my community. I teach classes and give interviews, sharing what I know. But something is missing. I feel guilty because I should be very grateful with the rich abundance I have in my work. I feel the need to reach out to more people and share with them what I have learned, people who yearn for the spiritual, to find meaning, to understand why things happen the way they do.

I summarized my question like this; "What next step should I take in my work?"

Here's the dream I received: I am being led down a corridor by two golden angels. I ask them where we are going. They inform me that they are taking me to a class about "what God wants you to do." I tell them that I am very excited about this class. I have been praying about this for a long time. I thank them for accompanying me. We reach the classroom door. One angel points to the workshop sign on the door. The title of the class is printed on it. It says, "Directions From God." The other angel begins to gently shake me. She says, "Wake up now and write that down. That's the subject for your book."

This book is the result of that dream. It is not intended to be a book about what I think God wants you to do. It also is not a book about my conversations with God. This book is about listening, feeling, and experiencing God's presence through your divine birthright – your intuition.

People call God by many names: Higher Consciousness, the Universe, Divine Wisdom, to name but a few. Every person has a unique sense of the meaning of the word "God." To me, the concept of God means an invisible intelligence that animates our world and provides wisdom and love to guide our lives.

I have often joked that we should arrive with an instruction manual from God about our life's purpose. Or we should be given a tape like the one in the old television series, "Mission Impossible," "Here is your mission should you choose to accept it!" However, over the years I have come to believe that we do in fact receive this guide to life. It comes through the whispers of our soul by means of our intuition. As you listen to the "guidance within," will you not only hear the directions you need for creating a life of peace and meaning, but you will also find you receive ample instructions for living the life of your dreams.

In my own background this is how these instructions came to me: I had been trying to figure out a career for myself for many years. During my 20s I had worked in a number of non-profit organizations. In my early 30s I worked as the Operations Manager of a software company.

I always wanted to be self-employed. I wanted to be my own boss, make my own hours, and have some degree of financial independence. I certainly wanted to make more money than I was making in the non-profit organizations in which I worked. I started asking myself questions. What is it that I love? What would my ideal work situation look like? What hobbies and interests do I have that I could use to make a living? How much money would I like to make? I wrote all this down and came up with this list:

I like counseling people. I like to study metaphysics and consciousness. I am a good listener. I like to teach. I want to work for myself. I like to write.

I toyed with the idea of becoming a psychologist. I sent for some applications and went on a few interviews. I felt very let down and disappointed after doing this. Everything felt heavy about it. Because I believe that intuition often speaks to us through feelings and body sensations. That sense of heaviness indicated to me that counseling was not a good choice for me.

I thought about becoming a psychic. I took classes on developing psychic abilities and found I had a great deal of natural talent in this area. My main concern was "How do I develop a psychic reading business??" I quipped that if God posted a "Psychic Reader Wanted" ad in the Sunday *Boston Globe* jobs section, I would apply. Barring that, I had no idea where to begin.

I had been studying metaphysics for many years. The basic theory of this philosophy is that whatever you focus your attention on tends to manifest in some way in your life. I thought about how I could apply this to my desire for a new career. I knew the outcome of what I wanted; I just didn't know how to get there! I decided to go to work with my understanding of practical metaphysics. I wanted to see if I could get some assistance from what I affectionately call "The Helpers of the Universe." (I give you more on that later.)

My goal: "I have a full-time, successful psychic reading business."

My visualizations: 1) My appointment book is full of clients. 2) I see a happy client sitting across from me as I give a psychic reading. 3) I see my answering machine blinking with lots of messages from clients.

About a month into this manifesting process, a friend, who had been sick for a long time, died. As I walked into the room for his funeral service I felt a strong inclination to sit next to a woman I had not met before. There were quite a few people in the room that I both knew and preferred to sit next to for emotional support but the feeling was so strong, I took the seat next to the stranger.

At the end of the service the woman and I started talking and she asked me what I did for a living. Have you ever had one of those times where your brain doesn't engage with your mouth? Despite the fact that my job at the time was Operations Manager, I answered, "I'm a psychic." I was immediately stricken with alarm. "Why had I answered this way? What would she think?!" I had done readings for a few friends and friends of friends. But I never defined my career that way! I felt flustered by my answer, but to my surprise she was quite open and receptive. She then told me that she was a writer for the *Boston Globe* and would love to have a reading so she could write about it in her column.

We arranged a time that I would go to her house to give her a reading. I was so nervous! What if I blew it?! What if I didn't get any information?

What if she hated what I said? What if I was wrong? I was in quite a state when I arrived at her home. Despite my anxiety, as soon as I started the session a remarkable peace came over me. The information flowed very easily and effortlessly and she was really pleased.

She called a few weeks later to say that she had written a piece about our session for the paper. She wanted to tell me not to be disappointed if it did not appear in her column. She was pretty sure her editor would not accept it, mostly because of the topic but also because the editor usually did not allow articles about specific individuals in the column. A few days later she called again, leaving the message that her editor was enthusiastic about the story and agreed to run it!

Here's what Mopsey Strange Kennedy wrote in an article entitled, "Psychic Psychology" in the *Boston Globe* on June 21, 1987:

Whatever one's vision of a psychic might be, Lynn Robinson is probably not it. There is a practical quality to what she offers, and at the same time she has been known to have some extraordinary "seeings" into the specifics of a client's life. Once associated with Interface, a holistic center, Robinson has what might be loosely called a perspective of spiritual psychology. She can be descriptive and explanatory about a situation or relationship, but she's not above occasional direct suggestions. Her findings are most concerned with addressing the rhythms of a person's life, understanding the stubborn blocks and flowing places where that thing called growth might take place. Her insights partake of a Zen-like suppleness that allows for flexibility and grace, even in the presence of what might be unsettling or painful.

Within the next six months I received over 400 calls from this one article. Most of these people made appointments – my business was launched. My goal had come true in a way I could never have arranged if left to my own devices. I had a successful psychic reading business! Then it hit me… I had joked that I wanted God to post a "psychic reader" position in the *Boston Globe*. It had happened! It just wasn't in the "Help Wanted" section.

That is my story of how one of my dreams came true with help from the Universe. This book is about helping you learn how to access the rich wisdom available to you through your gift of intuition. My hope is that I can help you receive your directions from God so you can live your life with enthusiasm and joy. Let's get started.

Lynn A. Robinson

"FOR THE SPIRITUAL BEING, INTUITION IS FAR MORE THAN A HUNCH. IT IS VIEWED AS GUIDANCE OR AS GOD TALKING, AND THIS INNER INSIGHT IS NEVER TAKEN LIGHTLY OR IGNORED."

WAYNE DYER

DIVINE INTUITION: DIRECTIONS FROM GOD?

You've picked up this book for any number of reasons. Someone told you they liked it. You may have heard me on the radio or on television. Perhaps you feel lost and need some direction and this book says it can help you "Create a Life You Love." If you are one of the 95% of people who believe in God, you may be suspicious of what "Divine Intuition" means, or what that has to do with God. But who or what is God? What does He, She, or It have to do with intuition and bettering your life? Asking these questions is a great place to start.

Everyone has a belief about God, even if one is a devout atheist who believes God doesn't exist. What's your vision of God? Is it an old man in a white robe sitting on a throne in some vast unseen place in the universe? Do you believe that life is an accident and you just happen to be here by chance and then you die? Maybe you believe there is a purpose in your being here and you haven't been able to figure it out. Perhaps you wish desperately that life came with a set of rules.

So how do you know God exists? You may have read many books on the subject of God and religion. You may have read none at all. The understanding I have of Divine Intuition might help you find some answers.

I am not a biblical scholar or a religion expert. I come from a Christian family that viewed church and Sunday school as something you did on religious holidays, which is to say that I didn't grow up in a deeply religious or spiritual home. I've come to my understanding of God through almost twenty years' experience as an intuitive counselor.

I've spoken to thousands of individual clients and students about the meaning of their lives and life in general. I've seen people struggle with concerns of being punished by an unforgiving and vindictive God. I've seen others embrace God as a loving, positive source of comfort and guidance. Still others

"SILENCE IS THE LANGUAGE GOD SPEAKS, AND EVERYTHING ELSE IS A BAD TRANSLATION."

FATHER THOMAS KEATING

have no belief in God and yet experience difficulty with the idea of finding purpose and meaning.

My intention in writing this book is not to add yet another volume to the many books out there that proclaim, "I have the answer." My purpose is to assist you in finding your own answer. I believe the key to your destiny resides in your heart and soul. The power I call "God" placed it there and you can access it through your intuition or inner guidance.

I believe that God and God's wisdom is hard-wired into our genes and our reason for being. From time immemorial we have in some way, shape, or form worshipped a higher power. For as long as people have been on this planet, they have left traces of some greater energy, deity, God, or force.

GOD AS A POSITIVE FORCE

I believe that God exists as a positive force in all of our lives. I believe that it doesn't matter how you view God – as Goddess, Source of Life, Love, Divine Energy, Spirit, Life Potential, Universal Intelligence, or as a wise old man sitting on clouds surrounded by angels. We often personify what we can't see or understand. So for the purpose of this book, however, you view or experience "God" is fine. You may find value here even if you're a total non-believer. Marianne Williamson writes of God as "the pure and all-powerful love that rules the universe and lies within us all."

There is no one truth or right way to view God.

"THE FIRST WORD THAT COMES TO ME ABOUT THE EXPERIENCE OF GOD IS PEACE. I FEEL LOVED, I FEEL CARED FOR, AND PEACE COMES WITH THAT NO MATTER HOW DIFFICULT THE SITUATION."

BERNIE SIEGEL

"I WILL PUT MY LAW WITHIN THEM, AND I WILL WRITE IT UPON THEIR HEARTS."

JEREMIAH 31:33

Many will dispute that fact and claim to have "The Answer." Wars too numerous to count have been waged over who has the right belief about God. You will find your truth within. That's where God placed it.

AN ALL PERVADING ENERGY

My hope is that in these pages you find some comfort and direction. Whatever your belief is about the source, you have access to a deep inner wisdom that resides in your soul. Your intuition can summon the answers from this Divine Wisdom and help you live your life fully with your heart open and your arms flung wide.

The commonality I have found in the world religions is that we are counseled to love others, forgive, be of service, and to act with humility and compassion. People have experienced God in the wind, in a church or temple, in the trenches of a war, on the street, in a baby's eyes, in the last breath of a loved one, in their cars, offices, and even in a bar. God is an energy, an all-pervading spirit. He is truly everywhere – in our waking, in our sleeping, and in our dying.

Many of the more logical among you will point to the fact that I can't prove that God exists. It's true that I can't point to God's presence and say, "There He is. Right there!" However, I see signs of God everywhere. Universal Wisdom resides in the

"BY LISTENING TO THE CREATOR WITHIN, WE ARE LED TO OUR RIGHT PATH."

JULIA CAMERON

WHAT IS GOD?

Here are ten questions to ponder as you begin the book. Some of the answers may be clear to you now and some may become clearer as you read further.

◆

1) Have you ever experienced God's presence? If so, describe the experience.

◆

2) What were you taught about God as a child? Are your beliefs the same now? If not, how do they differ?

◆

3) What practices (such as praying, meditating or going to religious services) bring you closer to God?

◆

4) How do you envision God?

◆

5) What is the purpose of life?

◆

6) What takes you away from God?

◆

7) Do you pray or ask for guidance in some other way?

◆

8) If yes, how do you receive the answer?

◆

9) What do you think God wants you to learn in this life, if anything?

◆

10) What name do you give God?

daffodil that knows to blossom in the spring when the earth is warming. God's love is in my neighbor's heart when she brings over dinner when I return from a long trip. I feel the presence of Spirit when I hear the children laughing as they ride their bikes outside my house. I witness the protection of the Goddess when my friend gives birth to her son.

Most importantly, through your intuition you gain enlightenment and direction from All-That-Is, which is what I call God. That wisdom is part of you and though you can't touch it or see it, you can experience it. It's there and it's real. My hope is that through this book it will become alive for you and you may use it to create a life you love.

"THE INTELLECT HAS LITTLE TO DO ON THE ROAD TO DISCOVERY. THERE COMES A LEAP IN CONSCIOUSNESS, CALL IT INTUITION OR WHAT YOU WILL, AND THE SOLUTION COMES TO YOU, AND YOU DON'T KNOW HOW OR WHY."

ALBERT EINSTEIN

THE GIFT OF INTUITION

I believe that each of you has chosen to come into this life with a mission. It's your purpose in life. It's the thing that brings joy and enthusiasm. The root of the word enthusiasm is entheos. *It literally means "God Within." Think for a moment about what that really means. When you feel enthusiastic about your dreams it means that God is speaking through you and saying "yes" to your goals! The feeling of enthusiasm is one of the ways intuition speaks to us.*

THE MUSICIAN, KENNY LOGGINS ONCE OBSERVED "FEELING IS GOD'S MIRROR; INTUITION IS GOD'S TELEPHONE." I know from personal experience and from working with my clients and students, that intuition is an unwavering and reliable source of wisdom to guide our lives. It is an inner resource that gives us unfailing direction towards our hopes and dreams. Fortunately, everyone has it, and all are all capable of developing it for practical use in everyday life as well as for discovering and achieving life goals.

Many people think of intuition as the domain of a gifted few, even though it's now recognized not as a rare, accidental talent, but as a natural ability all have and anyone can develop. I believe the world will be a far better place to live when we all know how to routinely use the gift of intuition to enhance the quality of our lives.

We've all heard the admonition to "Follow your heart." "Listen to your inner voice." "Trust your guidance." These are all ways that we receive intuitive guidance. These common phrases make it sound so easy. But what do you do when your inner voice sounds like your inner critic, or worse, your inner child run amok? How can you learn to distinguish between your own inner knowing (your intuition) and your deepest inner fears?

Webster's defines intuition as "quick and ready insight;" and "the act or process of coming to direct knowledge without reasoning or inferring." It is derived from the Latin word "intueri" which means "to see within." It is a way of knowing, of sensing the truth without explanations. My favorite

> **"WHEN WE COMBINE THOUGHT WITH FEELING, INTELLECT WITH EMOTION, AND ADD TO THIS A RECOGNITION OF GOD WITHIN, WE HAVE A POWER THAT IS IRRESISTIBLE."**
>
> SCIENCE OF MIND

definition of intuition is from a 15-year-old girl who said, "Intuition is like when you know something, but like, where did it come from?"

GAIN VALUABLE INSIGHT

Intuition is a resource that provides an additional level of information that does not come from the analytical, logical, and rational side of the brain. It can be a reliable and valuable tool when its language is understood and developed. Accurate intuition enables you to gain vital and valuable insight into yourself, your children, friends, business associates, and the world around you. Even more importantly, as you'll come to see in this book, it provides you with guidance so that you can recognize and nurture the thoughts and actions that will achieve your hopes and dreams.

Psychologist Carl Jung calls intuition one of the four basic psychological functions, along with thinking, feeling, and sensation. He describes it as the function that "explores the unknown and senses possibilities and implications which may not be readily apparent."

Why is it important to listen to your intuition? When you listen to your intuition it connects you with a great knowledge, that part of you with an overview of your life that has your best interest at heart. It can provide an oasis of peace in the midst of chaos, bring you to harmony, help you release judgments, and give you confidence to take action and prepare for change in your life. It also can be a valuable guide as you take steps to create your dreams.

Developing intuition is like learning to develop any skill, whether it be mastering a new computer software program or becoming proficient at a musical instrument. That is, the more you use your intuition the better you get at it. Intuition becomes second nature when you practice it. If you use intuition regularly you will develop an "instant knowing." This sixth sense, the hunch, the gut feeling becomes a sure thing and can be trusted and relied on when making decisions.

> **"THERE'S AN INVISIBLE ORGANIZING INTELLIGENCE THAT WE'RE ALL PART OF, AND WE'RE ALL HERE FOR A REASON."**
>
> WAYNE DYER

> **"WHAT IS TRUTH? A DIFFICULT QUESTION; BUT I HAVE SOLVED IT FOR MYSELF BY SAYING THAT IT IS WHAT THE VOICE WITHIN TELLS YOU."**
>
> MAHATMA GANDHI

How You Receive Intuition

Intuition can take on many forms: images, symbolic pictures, vivid dreams. For example, a designer who receives visual impressions might "see" the solution to a product design problem as a series of images relating to the product.

Intuitive impressions may also be experienced kinesthetically. These impressions might be felt as emotions, a sense of direct knowing, a hot or cold sensation in the body, or a gut feeling. For example, an intuitive therapist might receive impressions by "feeling" the direction she needs to take with her client.

Another way of receiving information is verbal. You might hear words in your mind or find that your intuitive answers are formed as metaphors or symbols. You "hear" the words telling you a new direction to take. In an example I used in the Introduction, I "heard" the direction to "sit there" next to the woman at the funeral service for my friend. There is no single, "right" way to experience intuitive information. How it is

> **"INTUITIVE KNOWLEDGE IS AN ILLUMINATION OF THE SOUL, WHEREBY IT BEHOLDS IN THE LIGHT OF GOD THOSE THINGS WHICH IT PLEASES HIM TO REVEAL TO US BY A DIRECT IMPRESSION OF DIVINE CLEARNESS."**
>
> RENÉ DESCARTES

SIXTY SECONDS TO PEACE

Here's a very simple exercise to get you started. I call this my "One-Minute God" exercise." So many of us claim to not have the time it takes to sit down to pray or meditate. With this exercise, you don't really have an excuse! You'll find it quite effective.

◆

Close your eyes, take a deep breath in, and say the word "relax" as you slowly let your breath out. Do this several times until you feel yourself becoming calm and centered. Now, simply call on the presence of God. There is no "right way" to do this. However you experience it is fine. Quiet your thoughts, let go of any anxious feelings, draw to yourself a sense of calm and peace. Take in this stillness with your in-breath. Let go of any concerns with your out-breath.

◆

Say to yourself, "I am filled and surrounded by the presence and spirit of God. I am at peace." Visualize the love and light of God enfolding you. Imagine that you are simply sitting in this energy and resting.

◆

This simple exercise done even a few times a day produces amazing recuperative results. It helps you change your perspective, clear away stress, and gain more energy. I've found that when I calm myself in this way intuitive insights will often pop into my mind. I seem to keep them away when I'm feeling stressed and driven.

developed and perceived is a matter of what works best for you.

Ernest Holmes, the founder of the Science of Mind Church says, "When the scientist listens, the artist imagines, the mathematician calculates, or the poet waits for the muse to guide fancy into word pictures, each is praying for divine guidance. And each receives as much guidance as he or she is capable of perceiving."

Throughout this book I will give you lots of exercises, tools, prayers, and food for thought to help you access this remarkable gift from Spirit. You were born with an inner guidance system that was designed to help you create the life of your dreams. Now all you have to do is discover it!

"TWENTY YEARS FROM NOW YOU WILL BE MORE DISAPPOINTED BY THE THINGS YOU DIDN'T DO THAN BY THE ONES YOU DID DO. SO THROW OFF THE BOWLINES. SAIL AWAY FROM THE SAFE HARBOR. CATCH THE TRADE WINDS IN YOUR SAIL. EXPLORE. DREAM. DISCOVER."

MARK TWAIN

MAKING YOUR DREAMS COME ALIVE

What's your dream? Have you forgotten it? Many of us do. You start out in this life with hopes and dreams and ambitions. Often they are quickly dissipated by your fears: What will people think? Can I earn enough money at it? How could I possibly attain this goal? I'm not good enough. I don't have the right education or enough money to attain my dream. You often talk yourself out of your goal before you've even begun. When you have a dream and are committed to achieving it, your life takes on new meaning. You have a purpose in life.

BY DISCOVERING AND UNFOLDING A DREAM, you feel excitement. What is it that makes you happy and brings you joy? It may be a small thing or big thing, you may love to garden, or to manage a corporation, or to care for babies. Through doing what you love, you draw in the energy of hope, peace, and forgiveness. Gradually you learn to take small steps to create a life you love.

LISTENING TO GUIDANCE

"What do you see for me?" is the question I'm so frequently asked when I begin a session with a client. I translate that as "Please help me. I've forgotten my dream and I need some help in finding it again." Often we get caught up in complaining about what doesn't work in our lives. We forget to listen to the guidance, which we all receive, that can get us back on track.

Have you forgotten your dream? As a child you could probably fill your days with imagination, curiosity, wonder, and joy. What do you daydream about now? What do you think about when you're

LIMERICK COUNTY LIBRARY

> ❝REACH HIGH, FOR STARS LIE HIDDEN IN YOUR SOUL. DREAM DEEP, FOR EVERY DREAM PRECEDES THE GOAL.❞

PAMELA VAULL STARR

stopped at a traffic light or when you're lying in bed on a Sunday morning not having to leap out at the first ring of the alarm? Do you imagine what it would be like to start your own business? Maybe your dream would be to spend your days gardening. Your dream doesn't necessarily have to apply to your work or career. It may become a way that you see yourself earning a living, or it may simply be a hobby or an avocation.

Your dreams and hopes are part of your guidance system from what I call "God." I have often wished that the God I imagined as a child, the one with the flowing white beard sitting on a huge throne, would come down out of the sky and say to me, "LYNN ROBINSON, THIS IS YOUR PURPOSE IN LIFE!" Then he would hand me the script! Wouldn't it be easy if it worked that way? Yet the system for receiving these great "Divine Messages" *is* built into each of us. It is "Intuition," and we all have it. I like to think of it as the Universe's e-mail!

STAY TRUE TO YOUR DREAMS

When I was a teenager, I was lost. I did not seem to have any idea of my life's ambitions. I grew up in a college town in western Massachusetts where everyone seemed to know what they wanted to be when they grew up. Most of my friends' parents were bright, well-educated people who taught at the local colleges and university. We were all expected to go to college and have successful, well-paying careers.

Choosing a college program is easier if you want to be something "normal" like an accountant, a teacher, or a marine biologist. What do you choose when you're fascinated by spirituality (but not organized religion), when you communicate with your spirit guides, and

love to read books about psychic abilities? When I was about 15 years old my mother must have been a bit concerned because she made an appointment for me with the high school guidance counselor. He was an old man (probably about 30!) and seemed to me very out of touch. He asked me questions about my interests and hobbies and what I liked in school. I think he didn't know what to do with me or what college program to recommend to a teenager with my set of interests. No suggestions were forthcoming, and I never saw him again. I gave up on my dreams because I couldn't figure out where to begin.

LIVE THE LIFE YOU DREAMED

A song recorded by Judy Collins says, "In the valleys you look for the mountains. In the mountains you've searched for the rivers. There is nowhere to go. You are where you belong. You can live the life you dreamed." But many of us don't believe it because, sadly, we have forgotten our dreams.

We feel that we have become increasingly overwhelmed in life. We seem to plan every last minute, so we need to treasure those pockets of time when we stop at a traffic light or just before falling asleep at night – use them to daydream. I'm a big believer in daydreams. My theory is that they inform you of what you need in your life.

To give you a very simple example, if you are spending a lot of time imagining what it would be like to enjoy a week at the beach reading trashy novels, it may be time for a vacation! Your guidance system informs you through this imagery. Your daydreams are usually pleasurable for a reason: they beckon you as if to say, "Try this." This is your intuition, in the form of daydreams, showing you some possible solutions to a problem or concern.

> ❝WHATEVER YOU CAN DO, OR DREAM YOU CAN, BEGIN IT. BOLDNESS HAS GENIUS, POWER AND MAGIC IN IT.❞

GOETHE

What if you knew for certain that everything you are presently worried about would work out okay? What if you knew that you had the inner wisdom to handle any life situation that came along, that even if something difficult came your way, you would still be okay, and that you had a constant source of abundance flowing to you at all times? What if you didn't have to worry? What would you do?

YOUR MAGNIFICENT GUIDANCE SYSTEM

Many people are out of practice with listening to their inner guidance systems. They have ignored the gentle "intuitive nudges" from their inner selves until they feel out of touch with their dreams. People receive this guidance in so many different ways. There is no ONE right way. Intuitive information might come through meditation, from a strong emotion, or simply "just knowing."

Imagine your own hopes and dreams. Is there something you really desire in your life? Perhaps a new job, a positive change in a relationship, or a business you would love to start. If you are like most people, you often feel swamped and do not know where to begin to achieve your inner goals. You may feel overwhelmed with options or feel like you have none at all. Either way, you find it difficult to decide which direcation to take.

You want to live your dreams, but keep putting it off, waiting for your circumstances to change. And they may. . . perhaps Ed McMahon from Publisher's Clearinghouse will drop by YOUR door and declare, "You just won . . .!" One day, you may actually have the time, money, and life circumstances that you have always wanted. You may even come to feel deserving of your dreams. Wouldn't that be wonderful?

But whether your circumstances change or not is unimportant. Pay attention to those dreams. They inform you about your life's purpose. Would it make sense for God to send people to Earth with the directions, "Stay focused on what makes you feel bad, negative, drained, and enervated?"

Fortunately human beings have been sent here with a magnificent inner guidance system. It is really quite simple to find; just ask: "What makes me happy, fills me with joy, or thrills me with excitement?" If you

WHAT INTUITIONS DO YOU HAVE?

Write a few sentences here or in your notebook about something you'd like intuitive guidance about. For example: Dear God — I'm ready to leave my present job and would like to (fill in your hope and dream). Please give me information through my intuition about the right path to follow. Thank you."

◆

Keep a small notebook with you throughout the day. When your intuition speaks, pay attention! Trust that your divine guidance will give you words, feelings, insights, and dreams that will guide you to the right path. At the end of each day look at your notes and see if a theme emerges that points you in a direction.

◆

Are you willing to act on the information? What could you do today to start making your dreams come alive? One way you can know that you're aligned with the Universe is that you feel more and more alive. Notice what gives you joy and excitement as well as what drains you. When you begin to say yes to your enthusiasms, you're on your way to making your dreams come alive. Trust that your divine guidance will not let you down. It will show you the way.

have those feelings about anything at all in your life, that is part of your guidance system telling you what to do.

START TODAY!

I suggest that at first you don't concern yourself with the question, "How can I make money by realizing this dream?" I am not suggesting that you immediately tell your boss to do as the song says — "Take This Job and Shove It!" I am asking you to pay attention to your daydreams. To begin to see them as directions from God that will guide you toward a happier life. None of these changes has to happen overnight. But why not start today? If you do, you might find that the very act of beginning can change your circumstances. Acting on your dreams is an important part of achieving your goals. As Will Rogers once observed, "Even if you're on the right track, you'll get run over if you just sit there."

"HERE'S THE GOOD NEWS: GOD IS A NAG. GOD WON'T GIVE UP. IF WE ARE DESTINED TO CARRY OUT SOME DIVINE IDEA, WE WON'T BE ABLE TO SHRUG IT OFF. FOR ME, GOD DOESN'T JUST WHISPER WITHIN. IF I'M SUPPOSED TO GET A MESSAGE, I START TO SEE IT AND HEAR IT EVERYWHERE – BOOKS, SERMONS, TELEVISION SHOWS, CONVERSATIONS WITH FRIENDS."

ELLEN DEBENPORT

INTUITIVE NUDGES

It has been said that coincidences are God's way of remaining anonymous. We often have serendipity occurring in our lives as a way to show us we are on the right path. Intuition rarely gives you the message just once. If you miss the message the first time, you'll continue to hear, feel, and see what I call "Intuitive Nudges" toward the right path from your inner guidance system.

TAKE A MOMENT RIGHT NOW AND THINK OF A MAJOR CHANGE THAT YOU'VE MADE IN YOUR LIFE in the past five years. Can you remember some of the circumstances that led up to your decision to make this change? Most likely you had an initial inkling that this would be a good move for you. The more you investigated, researched, and took action, the better it felt. You began to notice things falling into place. Doors seemed to open for you; synchronicities began to occur. These are intuitive nudges. You are receiving a "YES!" from God.

IS YOUR DREAM BIG ENOUGH?

In Mary Manin Morrissey's wonderful book, *Building Your Field of Dreams*, she suggests you ask yourself five questions to determine if your dream, your goal, is big enough: "Does this dream enliven me? Does this dream align with my core values? Do I need help from a higher source to make this dream come true? Will this dream require me to grow into more of my true self? Will this dream ultimately bless others?"

When we have a dream, it is our intuitive guidance telling us there is something new and exciting for us to move towards. Our job is not to figure out all the steps necessary to reach that goal; it is to follow the guidance via the "intuitive nudges" that will lead us on the path to the attainment of our dream.

"GOD IS LOOKING FOR AN OPPORTUNITY TO REVEAL HIMSELF TO YOU, SO IF YOU PUT HIM TO THE TEST AND THEN WATCH FOR AN ANSWER WITHOUT TOO MANY PRECONCEPTIONS ABOUT HOW THAT ANSWER WILL COME, I CAN GUARANTEE THAT YOU'LL BE IN FOR SOME EXCITING SURPRISES."

PAT BOONE

THE FORMS INTUITIVE NUDGES TAKE

Your thoughts Sometimes a subtle shift in perception about a difficulty you are facing opens up a world of options that did not seem to exist previously. I remember a time when my business had been really slow for a few months. I was getting a bit panicky about it and prayed for some way to turn this around. I felt frustrated at the seeming lack of guidance I was getting when I tried to pray and meditate. I decided to go for a walk to see if I could get out of the depressed mood I was in. As I walked I thought about all the things I was grateful for in my life. As my mood began to lift and I felt more hopeful, marketing ideas for my business started to pop into my head. Before the end of the walk I had a plan of action. Within a few weeks of implementing the new concepts, I had several new clients.

Images/symbolic pictures Everyone is familiar with the old adage that a "picture is worth a thousand words." Your inner guidance system knows this too! Albert Einstein was a great believer in the power of intuition. He wrote that the elements in his creative solutions were often received through visual images and that "words or other signs had to be sought for laboriously." He used what he called "thought experiments" to arrive at solutions to highly complex problems. He had an image of a person riding a beam of light which allowed him the insight that gave birth to the theory of relativity. He also reported that many of the solutions he sought came to him while shaving!

Your dreams I've mentioned earlier that my business began seemingly overnight when an article appeared in the *Boston Globe*. I was still working at my job in a software company. Torn between leaving my job to do the readings full time or trying to do both at once, I was experiencing a lot of anxiety. "Can I do my software job and begin the psychic reading business at the same time?" was how I phrased my question to God in my prayers. I was still

thinking about this as I drifted off to sleep one night. I woke up the next morning, laughing. I had received the answer in my dreams. I dreamed that I was out on a lake and I was in "canoes." That's right. I had one foot in one canoe and the other foot in another canoe and they were both pointed in different directions! I gave notice at my job the next day and I haven't felt a moment of regret since.

Emotions Your guidance may also come in the form of a feeling or emotion. Many times I have been wrestling with a decision, "Should I choose this or should I choose that?" I can go around in circles in my mind trying to logically assess all the different possibilities that may spring from a certain choice. Often you have no practical way to ascertain whether a decision is the right one for you or not. What then? In the second *Star Wars* movie, *The Empire Strikes Back*, Luke Skywalker asks Yoda, his mentor, "How am I to know the good from the bad?" Yoda answers,: "You will know through peace and calm." Yoda's response is an intuitive one. Even when you are in the position

> **"I HAVE A SENSE OF DESTINY AS THOUGH MY LIFE WAS ASSIGNED TO ME BY FATE AND HAD TO BE FULFILLED. THIS GAVE ME AN INNER SECURITY… OFTEN I HAD THE FEELING THAT IN ALL DECISIVE MATTERS, I WAS NO LONGER AMONG MEN, BUT WAS ALONE WITH GOD."**
>
> C.G. JUNG

of making a difficult and painful decision, usually one choice brings some ease or "peace and calm" to resolve your dilemma.

Physical intuition Your body provides a wealth of guidance and feedback to you. Everyone has heard of a "gut feeling." The Japanese actually have an interesting word for it, "haragei," which loosely translated means "stomach art." How does your body feel when you have made a decision? Many people report a heaviness or a knot in their stomach when they are making a poor choice. You may experience a shiver of recognition, or a pulse of positive energy throughout your body when the decision you are making is moving you in the right direction. Your body may have other ways of communicating your intuitive knowing. By learning to pay attention to how your body feels it is possible to receive rich guidance about your choices and direction in life.

Other people Your intuition may guide you to others who may provide a solution to your concern. I recently spoke with a client, Carla, who was quite concerned about how her young son, Jay, was doing in his fifth grade class. She told me she and her husband were planning to separate and Jay was acting out in school as a result. For the past week, Carla had been praying about how to help him. She mentioned that she had been at the school recently and felt strongly guided to drop in on his second grade teacher. Carla confided to the woman what was happening in her family. The teacher mentioned that she had just started an after school-program for kids with family difficulties who needed extra tutoring and coaching and would love to have Jay in her program. This proved to be a wonderful answer to Carla's prayers. Jay came home from the first session bubbling with enthusiasm.

> "MY BELIEFS I TEST
> ON MY BODY,
> ON MY INTUITIONAL
> CONSCIOUSNESS,
> AND WHEN I GET
> A RESPONSE THERE,
> THEN I ACCEPT."
>
> D. H. LAWRENCE

THE WRITE DIRECTION

A technique that I often use for inner guidance is called "directed writing." Here are the steps:

✦

1) Begin by writing a few sentences about a challenge you are currently facing in your life.

_____

_____

_____

✦

2) Write a one sentence question that summarizes your concern. Word it in such a way that it evokes more than a "yes" or "no" answer. Examples: "How can I create more money?" or "What could I do to increase my intuition?"

_____

_____

_____

✦

3) With your notebook and pen on your lap, close your eyes. Use any technique that helps you comfortably get into a deeply relaxed state. You might use a mantra or count down from 10 to 1, or focus on your breath as you slowly breathe in and out.

✦

4) Imagine you are being filled and surrounded by light and love. Simply having the intention allows you to do it correctly. Take a few deep, relaxing breaths.

✦

5) Ask your question. Be willing to wait in silence until you get an answer. Intuition comes in many ways. You may hear words, receive a feeling, an image, a body sensation, or you may have the answer pop fully formed into your mind. Begin to write down any answers or impressions you receive. You may find as you write that more information comes to you. Many people report that they feel they are making this up. Yet, when they act on the information they receive, it moves them in a positive direction.

✦

6) Open your eyes and review what you've written. Is there any action you can take, however small, on this intuitive insight? What are you being "nudged" to do?

_____

_____

_____

_____

_____

_____

7) Keeping a journal of your directed writings and reviewing it from time to time can be helpful. You may be surprised in hindsight at the accuracy of your guidance.

✦

When we have a dream, we receive inner wisdom from many different avenues to help us achieve it.

"GOD SPEAKS TO US EVERY DAY ONLY WE DON'T KNOW HOW TO LISTEN."

MAHATMA GANDHI

HOW DO YOU KNOW WHEN IT'S GOD ON THE LINE?

How can you discover who you are and why you are here? Do you look outside for this guidance or look within? And what do you look for? Is that vague stirring in your belly your inner wisdom informing you about a new direction to take or is it something you had for dinner?

IT IS COMMON TO HAVE A GREAT DEAL OF DIFFICULTY DIFFERENTIATING FEARS, HOPES, DREAMS, AND WISHFUL THINKING from true guidance. It gets so complicated at times that you may begin to wish that God's call came with Caller I.D.!

I believe that it is human nature to try to find God's answer in various signs. Confess now: Haven't you done it? You might say, "If that traffic light turns green before I get to it then the answer I'm seeking must be 'yes.'" People try to find cosmic revelation in signs, symbols, patterns, and forms. Since ancient times we have reports of this. For example, in Babylonia a wise man or baru would study the organs of an animal and to find answers to questions about the future.

You have all had seemingly unanswerable questions floating in your minds at one time or another: "Why am I here?" "Who am I?" "Is there some larger purpose to my existence?" "What's the right thing to do in this situation?" "What changes should I make?" "How can I know if it is God speaking to me?" How do you know who you are and what you should do? Do you look

"THE MOST DELICIOUS EXPERIENCE OF GOD IS FEELING COMPLETELY HELD, SUPPORTED, AND INFUSED WITH A LOVE BEYOND WORDS: LIKE THE FEELING THAT THE PSALMIST WROTE OF: BEING HELD IN THE PALM OF GOD OR BEING WRAPPED IN THE WINGS OF ANGELS. SAFE AND CONTENT."

JOAN BORYSENKO

outside yourself for the guidance? Does your minister, rabbi, Buddha, Jesus, Mohammed, or other religious leader have the right answer? Is the correct answer in the *Bible*, the *Koran*, or other religious book? Is your best friend's assurance that you are on the right track necessarily the right answer for you? Do you look for signs? Do you experience a faint urge to go this way or that and end up doing nothing?

GUIDELINES FOR GUIDANCE

Many people believe that God's guidance stopped during biblical times – that the only wisdom God has provided comes from the *Bible*. If you spend any time reading the *Bible*, you can find lots of indications of God speaking to the famous historical characters and directing them in their lives. In today's world, if someone says, "God made me do it," we are apt to feel concerned for their mental health or for our own safety.

So now I am offering some "guidelines for guidance," although you may think I am stating this obvious. If you are receiving true direction from God, you will never be guided to hurt or injure someone in any way.

How and when do you know when you've received guidance from God? For one thing, here are some of the ways students in my classes have answered that question:

+ When I experience a synchronicity or coincidence, my next steps have a resounding "yes!".
+ A feeling of peace comes over me as I contemplate a course of action.

> **❝THEN WHEN ALL THINGS WERE WRAPPED IN DEEPEST SILENCE, TO ME WAS UTTERED THE HIDDEN WORD.❞**
>
> MEISTER ECKHART

> **❝EXPERIENCING GOD GIVES ME THE MOST PROFOUND FEELING OF LOVE, BEAUTY, AND AWE: AWARENESS OF BEING ONE WITH THE CREATOR AND CREATION; TOTAL TRUST AND INNER PEACE.❞**
>
> WILLIS HARMAN

+ I get a glimpse of the "larger picture" that is unfolding in my life.
+ I begin to have compassion, or I experience forgiveness toward someone I feel has hurt or betrayed me.
+ I hear lyrics to a song that I can't get out of my head that has relevance to my concerns.
+ I'm drawn to a book or I overhear a conversation and the words seem as though they were directly spoken to me in answer to my request for guidance.
+ I feel I received guidance from God when I shared my concerns with a friend and she listened and responded with true love and compassion.
+ I begin to feel grateful or have an attitude of appreciation for my life even though I may be going through a difficult time.
+ Insight that comes quickly into my mind after a prayer is usually the right guidance to follow.
+ If the message contains thoughts of hope, love, encouragement, wisdom, strength, and comfort, I know it's from God.

WHAT DOES IT MEAN TO FOLLOW A "SPIRITUAL PATH?"

Dan Wakefield defines it in his book, *How Do You Know When It's God*: "Perhaps 'following a spiritual path' simply means the effort to live in a decent, fruitful way with the talents and flaws you've been given and the circumstances you've been dealt (and dealt yourself), and attempting to do so by the light of some faith in God, a Higher Power, and/or religious tradition to guide you."

I believe that one of the ways that God communicates to you is through your feelings of excitement, passion, and desire. The word desire is composed of the Latin prefix de-, meaning "from," and sidus, meaning "star." Desire literally means "from the stars." People too often cast aside their hopes of living a life of fulfilled dreams. They ignore the prompting of their inner wisdom and think that desires are simply there out of selfishness or self-indulgence. What would change in your life if you began to see your hopes and dreams as a calling from God?

One of the biggest misconceptions I have noticed is that most people expect God's call to come to

> ❝LISTEN TO ME;
> KEEP SILENT,
> AND I WILL
> TEACH YOU WISDOM.❞
>
> JOB 33:33

them in some huge, flashy, "gotta get your attention" manner. Sometimes it happens that way. Usually it doesn't. "Thunder doesn't rent the sky," Rod Serling once said, "and a bony finger come down from the clouds and point at you, and a great voice boom, 'You! You're the anointed!'"

Most of the time God communicates through the proverbial still, small voice. You may also be presented with a feeling, a fleeting impression, or a symbolic flash of insight. God's interaction with you is through encouragement to do what's right, to listen to guidance, to love yourself and others, to join in community, to be authentic, and to forgive. When you grow to recognize the

❝VOICES – I THINK THEY MUST GO DEEPER INTO US THAN OTHER THINGS. I HAVE OFTEN FANCIED HEAVEN MIGHT BE MADE OF VOICES.❞

GEORGE ELIOT

many ways God communicates, you come to trust the wisdom.

What do you do if you are facing a challenging time in your life and do not know what path to take? Perhaps you are struggling over whether to embark on a new career or wondering how you can be a better parent to your difficult child. Whatever difficulties you encounter, know that your answers exist within you. Author and minister Mary Manin Morrissey claims, "God imbued us with perfect truth meters that we can trust, when we are still, and really listen to the voice for God within."

The loving presence of God fills you with wisdom and informs your thoughts and actions,

"WHAT DOES GOD FEEL LIKE?…AT SUCH MOMENTS, MY BODY GOES THROUGH CHANGES – TINGLING, OPENING, LIGHTNESS, FEELING CONNECTED TO EVERYTHING. THERE'S A SENSE OF CLARITY ABOUT WHAT I SHOULD DO. THERE'S A SENSE OF COMPLETENESS, GRACE, AND SEAMLESS ACTION."

GURUCHARAN SINGH KHALSA

THE "YES!" RESPONSE

Here's a technique I use to help me clarify the direction from my intuitive guidance.

◆

1) Use your journal to write as much as you need to on what you're feeling upset about. When you feel that you've gotten it all down, you can proceed to the next step.

◆

2) What outcome do you want? Examples of this could be:
• I want to have a healthy body.
• I want to create a harmonious relationship with my ex-husband.
• I want to have work that's fun, rewarding, and pays well.
• I want to feel at peace about this issue.

◆

3) What are five options I have that will lead me to the outcome I want?

◆

4) Sit quietly and think about each of these options one at a time. At least one of them will call out to you and say, "Yes, this is right." You may experience this as a feeling in your body, a sense of peace or calm, as "yes!" spoken in your inner hearing, as a symbolic sign indicating a positive response. These are all ways your guidance communicates with you.

◆

5) Take action on this option.

encouraging you to love, forgive, be of service, have compassion, and fully live a life you love. You receive guidance from God toward these goals every moment of the day whether you are aware of it or not. You may be so caught in the habit of automatically doubting or contradicting it that you don't even know how to pay attention to it anymore.

Ask for guidance from God. State your intentions and ask for help if you are having difficulties. Spend time each day listening for guidance, meditating, or simply imagining yourself in the flow of Spirit and Divine Wisdom. Always make time in your life to do something that makes you happy and full of joy. This has more of an effect on your peace of mind than any other single factor. When you can experience peace during a difficult time, you will know you truly have God "on the line."

"PARACHUTES WEREN'T PROVEN TRUSTWORTHY BY HAVING PEOPLE CARRY THEM AROUND ON THEIR BACKS. THE DEVICE SHOWED ITS RELIABILITY ONCE SOMEONE JUMPED. GOD, TOO, CAN BE TRUSTED WITH OUR LIVES, WHICH WE DISCOVER ONCE WE TAKE A LEAP OF FAITH."

MARY MANIN MORRISSEY

TRUST IN DIVINE ORDER

Maybe you are beginning to feel as Mother Theresa once did when she said, "I know God will not give me anything I can't handle. I just wish that He didn't trust me so much." The Universe has a perfect plan for your growth and unfolding as a human being. In my readings for clients, I often receive a symbolic image of what appears to be a jigsaw puzzle that fills the entire cosmos. I am reminded when I see it that everyone has a piece of this puzzle that they contribute. There is a larger Universal blueprint for the unfolding of the individual's soul growth as well as for the human species.

HUMAN BEINGS ARE WIRED TO RECEIVE WISDOM AND GUIDANCE FROM GOD. When a person learns how to listen to intuition, that person hears the guidance that shows the next step to take. You do not have to be concerned with all the details about how to reach these goals and visions. You only need to be concerned about listening for the next steps.

LET GO AND LET GOD

You have probably read the words, "Let go and let God." What is this trust all about? Does it mean that you have no role or any responsibility for action in this process? Letting it go to God always sounded so passive to me, it used to make me anxious. Rather than helping me, I thought of it as giving up on what I wanted. But that is not trust at all.

To trust in God is to believe that there is a friendly, abundant, loving, wise energy that supports you and wants what is best for you. Letting your fears, concerns, wishes, and prayers "go to God" means that you trust in and work with this energy. God will work with you through your own built-in guidance system to help you draw to yourself what you want.

I am most comfortable when I am taking action on something. The concept of seeming to "do nothing" except let go to God has been a tough one to understand and accept. Here is a technique I use when I have been struggling with an issue without results. When you find yourself beginning to worry about an issue at any point in the day or night, remind yourself that you have let go of this concern and that you will receive guidance to resolve the problem.

As you listen for guidance on a daily basis you will find yourself being given one step at a time. The answer may come through an inspired idea, a dream, or a fleeting insight for new directions. When you consistently look within, asking, "What is the right course of action?" or "What path should I take?" you will be rewarded with wise divine guidance. It will always be there gracing your steps through life. You will find that your fear begins to drop away as you move forward with confidence in all your endeavors.

GOD IN DAILY LIFE

Go with what your inner guidance directs you to do. Sometimes this takes faith and courage. Begin with small steps. As you continue to trust this insight you will come to understand that your life's purpose and mission is unfolding. An invisible intelligence truly is leading and guiding you to a more peaceful and harmonious life.

Following is a prayer from an anonymous author that I find helpful when I'm going through a difficult time:

"Today I am going to surrender my concerns and difficulties to God. I will rest in the silence and know that confusion will fall away. I will rest in the peace that I feel. I will have the courage to take the right action. I will feel at peace knowing that the way has been made clear. Amen."

Here are some of the basic assumptions I make about God's role in my life:

* There is a wise, loving, and intelligent energy that I call God. This energy flows through me and through all of the universe.
* I may not be able to see this energy, but I choose to believe that God exists and has my best interest at heart.
* I believe that God informs me through my intuition about my best and highest direction. This guidance, if followed, leads me to greater peace and harmony in all aspects of my life.
* I believe that part of what God wants from each human being is to learn to love and be loved. God wants people to be kind, tolerant, and compassionate. Ultimately we come to understand that through our caring interdependence we can survive and flourish.

THE SURRENDER BOX

Write out your worry or concern on a 3 x 5 card. Here is an example: "Dear God – I'm having a difficult time communicating with Rose, my ex-wife, regarding our daughter. I need a new way to open up the dialogue between us and I feel stuck. Everything I've tried hasn't worked. I am surrendering this concern to You and asking for divine guidance to bring about healing."

✦

Summarize your concern with a question. "How can I communicate more effectively with Rose?"

✦

Close your eyes and go to your inner sanctuary or to the place of peace inside yourself. Take a few slow deep breaths until you feel your energy begin to shift.

✦

Call God to you. Imagine being in the presence of incredible love, light, and wisdom.

✦

Repeat the concern that you wrote on the card. Ask your question. Listen for any words, feelings, images, or sudden insights. Maintain a respectful silence, allowing any wisdom or guidance to enter your consciousness. Sometimes a new option will emerge out of the quiet.

✦

When you feel ready, imagine placing this concern in a bubble of light. See it being released into the universe. Know that you will receive further information to help you resolve this issue.

✦

Place your card in a box and place it on a shelf where you will see it frequently. I have my box decorated with the words "Surrender" on it.

"SITTING QUIETLY, DOING NOTHING, SPRING COMES AND GRASS GROWS BY ITSELF."

JAPANESE ZEN POEM

✦ There are many paths to finding and experiencing God. You may do it through prayer and meditation, or you may be someone who feels God's presence most strongly in nature, music, dancing, or art. Some people feel their connection to God through commitment to their spouses, children, and their families, or through service in their communities.

YOU ARE NOT ALONE

I have found a big secret over the 20 years or so that I have been giving readings. The secret is that everyone has had a dark time. I have not found anyone who has not. Along your spiritual path, you are likely to fall into a sort of wasteland. These desolate places in your being do not always show up in ways that the casual observer can detect. You tend to assume that everyone else is just fine and has not gone through the fears, shame, guilt, and humiliation that you have experienced.

How would you describe the time and the circumstances of your dark night of the soul? It might have been a series of failed relationships or an adulterous affair. A financial, job, or business loss may have plunged you into despair. You or a loved one may have gone through a health crisis. You may have felt that God had forsaken you at the time. Everyone has felt lost and abandoned, but it is during these times in the desert that God expands the soul, allowing it to hold more wisdom and love.

It is hard for people to understand why bad or difficult things happen when each person is trying to be good and to do what is right. The test is to believe definitely and consistently that the Universe is on your side. Author and minister Marianne Williamson put it succinctly, "The challenge is always to surrender our own will, to ask God to use us in service of healing the world, and to think with love toward all life. The Universe is always listening."

"DON'T TRY TO FORCE ANYTHING. LET LIFE BE A DEEP LET-GO. SEE GOD OPENING MILLIONS OF FLOWERS EVERYDAY WITHOUT FORCING THE BUDS."

BHAGWAN SHREE RAJNEESH

"I WILL GO BEFORE YOU, AND MAKE THE CROOKED PLACES STRAIGHT"

ISAIAH 45:2

A CLEAR PATH TO A POSITIVE LIFE

When you were a child you probably had a much clearer idea about what made you happy. You were willing to try new things and take risks without too much thought. As you got older you probably felt a lot of restrictions, eventually feeling very out-of-touch with your true calling and purpose in life. You may have made a practice of overriding your inner messages in search of more pragmatic visions. Because of this, you may feel that you have no idea what you want or what would truly make you happy. You feel you are going nowhere and getting there all too quickly!

YOU KNOW THAT YOUR LIFE NEEDS TO CHANGE. PERHAPS YOU ARE IN A RUT, bored, or just have a desire to do something new, and you are willing to try anything! The truth is we need challenge to thrive. How do you begin to figure out where to start when you do not know where you are going? One theory is that you already know what you want and need, but you probably have a bad case of what I call the "yesbuts."

Here are a few examples of "yesbuts" I have heard from my clients: "I love to learn about healing. I'm always taking classes and reading books about it. It fascinates me. But, I couldn't make a living at it." Or "If I could go shopping every day I would be in heaven. I love fashion and color and love to advise my friends on their outfits. But, I've decided to go to business school because I can't shop and make money!" Both of these people had clear access to their dreams and passions, but initially chose to ignore those inner messages for what appeared to be something more practical.

WHAT MAKES YOU HAPPY?

While it may seem like an odd "direction from God" – to love shopping as part of your mission in life – I will tell you the end of the story. The client, who I'll call Kay, ended up choosing to be an image consultant. In addition to working with executives, helping them to choose clothes and styles that fit their professional image, she also works with

> **"ATTITUDE IS MORE IMPORTANT THAN THE PAST, THAN EDUCATION, THAN MONEY, THAN CIRCUMSTANCES, THAN WHAT PEOPLE DO OR SAY. IT IS MORE IMPORTANT THAN APPEARANCE, GIFTEDNESS, OR SKILL. THE REMARKABLE THING IS, WE HAVE A CHOICE EVERYDAY REGARDING THE ATTITUDE WE WILL EMBRACE FOR THAT DAY. WE CANNOT CHANGE OUR PAST. WE CANNOT CHANGE THE FACT THAT PEOPLE ACT IN A CERTAIN WAY. WE CANNOT CHANGE THE INEVITABLE. THE ONLY THING WE CAN DO IS PLAY ON THE ONE STRING WE HAVE, AND THAT IS OUR ATTITUDE."**

CHARLES SWINDOLL

women who are getting off welfare. Kay gives seminars in self-confidence, interview skills, and dressing for success. Kay is someone who overcame her "yesbuts," trusted her intuition through the excitement that she felt, and created a wonderful business by serving others — which enabled her to make money at something she loved.

Our culture focuses on what is wrong. For instance, when was the last time you heard of massive research funding for studying healthy, happy people? When was the last time you went to a therapist who asked, "What makes you happy?" Have you ever gone to a doctor who congratulated you on all the things that were working well with your body?

STAY CENTERED IN THE PRESENT

If you agree that what you focus on with your thoughts and beliefs is intensified in your life, why not put all your attention on what makes you happy, challenged, and healthy? One of the techniques that works for me when I am feeling upset is simply to ask myself, "Is there another way to think about this issue?" I catch myself in the early stages of worry and negative thinking and begin to focus on what I want instead of what I don't want.

Do you know that it is perfectly normal to feel resistance or anxiety when you attempt something new? I always feel it. I used to think it meant I should not do the thing I was contemplating. I have a tendency to think too far into the future, and I get easily overwhelmed about how to get there from here.

The trick to breaking this habit of thought that afflicts many of us is two-fold: 1) just begin and 2) start small. Take a first step to what you feel excited about and then take another one and another one. Remain centered in the present. That is your point of power. Trust your inner direction from your intuition. When you follow your passion, excitement, and inner knowledge, you discover what makes you happy and fulfilled. When you know what you want, you find a clear path to achieving it. Your guidance shows you the way.

I have found that many people take the path of least resistance. You are out of work and when a job is offered, you think, "I might as well take it." You may have heard the saying, "If you don't know where you're going you'll probably end up there." It holds true in so many situations in your life. You need to check in with your inner guidance and ask, "Is this a good decision?" How will you know if you don't ask?

USE YOUR INTUITION FOR DECISIONS

I want you to try something new. Think of a decision you need to make. This could be a career decision, or an issue you are facing in a relationship, or perhaps new place where you may decide to live. On a piece of paper write two possible choices that you are considering. You may have more options available to you, but for the sake of the exercise just choose two. Now ask the question, "Where will this decision lead?" Underneath each of these choices write anything that comes to you. Do not discard any piece of information as irrelevant. Remember that God's wisdom comes in words, feelings, body sensations, images, or simple knowing. Look at the example I have given and then use your intuition on a choice or decision you need to make.

Daniel Wakefield wrote a wonderful line in his book, *How Do We Know When It's God?*: "If only God would speak to us, boom out instructions from a voice on high, we would gladly go into battle or up the mountain or into the rushing path of charging horses or foaming seas. If only we knew. For sure. The way."

> ❝PEACE COMES
> FROM WITHIN.
> DO NOT SEEK IT
> WITHOUT.❞
>
> BUDDHA

FEEL THE SPIRIT

1) Example of Choice A: I will take the job at Noname Corporation. I feel discouraged, let down, and my body feels heavy. I experience a slight knot in my stomach. I imagine myself at the company and my body feels prickly.

◆

2) Example of Choice B: I will keep looking for another job. I feel a little more hopeful. I am aware of feeling impatient. I want a resolution to my work situation. I have some ideas about people to call that just occurred to me. I feel lighter with this option.

◆

3) List two of your choices or decisions here and try the exercise yourself.

◆

4) What direction is your intuition giving you?

◆

Notice that you probably did not hear a booming voice of God saying, "This is the right decision! Take that job!" Everyone has free will. Inner guidance will lead to a path of more peace, joy, hope, and a positive life if only you learn to check in with it and follow its wisdom.

When you learn to check in consistently with your inner wisdom, the information you receive will be just as valuable and as reliable as if God were speaking with a booming voice from on high. To take the first step on the clear path to a positive life, you must begin to ask and listen.

When you think of someone who has "spirit," you probably think of someone with an abundance of positive and creative energy. They seem to be alive with purposefulness and have an aura of both security and serenity. We all have the power to create a positive life. Deep inside yourself, you have the road map to create that life. When you look within and find the glimmerings of what brings you energy, passion, and joy, you see the beginning of your path. Start to say "Yes" to those inklings, even though you do not know where that path will take you. Called faith and trust, those are qualities we all must embrace if we are to hear our directions from God.

"AS YOU BEGIN TO LIVE
IN THE PRESENT MOMENT,
YOU WILL EXPERIENCE A
SUBTLE BUT PROFOUND
CHANGE. WORRYING
ABOUT THE FUTURE WILL
CEASE. A DEEP PEACE
WILL ENFOLD YOU, A
PEACE THAT SAYS, 'ALL IS
WELL. THERE IS NOTHING
TO FEAR. EVERYTHING IS
UNFOLDING ACCORDING
TO PLAN, AND YOU ARE
BEING GUIDED EACH STEP
ALONG THE WAY. "

DOUGLAS BLOCH

WHAT DO YOU SAY WHEN YOU TALK TO YOURSELF?

Many successful people confess to me that they spend time daydreaming about their futures. They tell themselves positive statements about their lives and their ability to achieve goals. They envision successful outcomes of their goals and dreams. They anticipate abundance coming to them through the actions they take. All have very different goals or values, but they see themselves as being able to achieve success in any of their endeavors.

PERHAPS POSITIVE THINKING SEEMS LIKE A FAIRLY BASIC THING to you, but for many people it is not. I see clients who, when asked if they understand the importance of positive affirmations, would reply in so many words, "Yes! I'm positive things won't work out!"

Take just a moment and think about what you want to create in your life....

Were you able to do it? Changing your thoughts away from what you do not want to a focus on your hopes, dreams, and ambitions is a powerful shift in perspective. What do you say when you talk to yourself? Your self-talk determines the direction you go and the results you achieve in your life.

OPPORTUNITIES ARE COMING YOUR WAY

I read an article recently where the writer proclaimed, "If worrying were a paying job, I'd be a rich woman." I used to be that way, and I have to say I didn't create much prosperity while doing it! I worried constantly about whether I had enough money, or whether I was doing a good enough job at work, or whether people liked me. I believed that if I worried enough, the things I worried about wouldn't happen! But, in fact, focusing on what you do not want is a key component in keeping you stuck in a cycle of worry.

Have you ever felt "sick with worry?" I was constantly in a state of anxiety because of what I was telling myself. I was continually focusing on what I did not want to happen, and I was filled with fear. I finally sat down to meditate one evening after a particularly difficult day. I went to my inner sanctuary in my mind and asked my guide, "How can I let go of the anxiety I'm feeling?" The answer I received seemed deceptively simple. My guide responded, "Your lesson right now is to not worry." I remember coming out of meditation thinking, "Humph! Easy for her to say!" Yet I was so desperate I was willing to try.

I decided to give myself an initial time frame of one week. (You could try this for one hour at a time if you are a particularly chronic worrier.) I would have a worry thought come up such as, "I don't have enough clients scheduled for this week. What if my business is starting to fail? What if I won't have enough money this month?" I could feel myself begin to go into a downward spiral of panic and worry as more and more anxious thoughts piled up on the original one. Then I would remember my inner guide's message and manage to stop the worry and replace it with another attitude. My daily affirmation was, "Lynn, calm down. This is going to work out okay. New opportunities are coming your way. Just be patient. Everything is unfolding in the right time. God is handling this. Your job is to not worry this week."

At the end of the week I felt calmer. I had even

"YOUR MIND CAN ONLY HOLD ONE THOUGHT AT A TIME. MAKE IT A POSITIVE AND CONSTRUCTIVE ONE."

H. JACKSON BROWN, JR.

received an invitation to teach a seminar, and a magazine was interested in publishing an article I'd proposed. New doors to opportunity had opened a crack, and I felt a bit more hopeful. I was even willing to try this 'Don't worry, be happy' experiment for an entire month at a time. I had to be very diligent in catching myself at the beginning of the worry cycle. I finally learned to turn my thinking around. I chose to focus on what I was grateful for and to dwell on what I wanted to create rather than what I feared would happen. The change to my peace of mind was astounding. The results that I ended up creating were equally surprising and fulfilling.

If you plant a bunch of squash seeds what do you expect to come up out of the ground? A squash plant, right? If you plant squash seeds and a tulip started growing you would be more than a bit unsettled. Think of your thoughts as seeds. What you plant in your mind grows and attracts like-minded thoughts and experiences. Whether you plant "seeds" of worry and fear or "seeds" of hope and joy in your mind, your life will bear the fruit of your thoughts.

WHAT DO YOU WANT TO CREATE?

When you pay attention to your thoughts, what do you hear yourself saying about your life? These are the beliefs you hold. Do you believe you have a right to be successful? Do you trust yourself to make good decisions for your future? Do you believe that other people want you to succeed? Do you believe there is a loving God that will support you in your decisions for change? Your thoughts, beliefs, and emotions have a huge impact on what you create in your life.

Soren Kierkegard said, "Our lives always express the result of our dominant thoughts." If you talk with people who are successful you will find that they make full use of their imagination to visualize their future. They might imagine how they will feel when they close a big deal. They commonly picture a wonderful, idyllic vacation and the abundance to savor it. They see the success they want to achieve in their mind's eye. They enjoy these visions of what they hope to create.

"IT IS NOT ENOUGH TO HAVE A GOOD MIND. THE MAIN THING IS TO USE IT WELL."

RENE DESCARTES

As they visualize, they practice what we have come to know as affirmations. Most of you are familiar with affirmations. These are positive statements you tell yourself about your life and the success you imagine is coming your way. The power of your mind to imagine success is a key to creating a life you love.

What would you like to create in your life? What are the interests in your life that bring you joy or make you feel excited? This is how your intuition, through your emotions, brings information to you about your life's direction. Simply put: if it feels exciting and enjoyable, take some steps towards it and test it out. If you feel upset or drained by something, figure out a way to change the situation or let it go entirely.

I initially found the concept of creating my life experiences through my thoughts and beliefs very difficult to understand. I mean, wasn't it simply true that I was always broke? Wasn't it simply true that I would never get a good job because I hadn't gone to college? Many of us argue for our limitations by saying things like, "You just can't trust people," or "That's just the way things are." "Things will never change." Even if you are having a hard time with this idea that your thoughts create your life experiences, give it a trial period of a few weeks to a few months, and then notice what happens when you willingly alter your beliefs.

Someone once observed that if you always do

"SPIRITUAL BEINGS DO NOT ALLOW THEIR THOUGHTS AND FEELINGS TO FLOW FROM THEIR ACTIONS, THEY UNDERSTAND THAT THEIR THOUGHTS CREATE THEIR PHYSICAL WORLD."

WAYNE DYER

what you have always done, you will always get what you have always gotten. (Follow that!?) In other words, some aspect of yourself needs to change in order to create a different outcome. If something is consistently not working out in your life, look to your beliefs via your self talk. What do you say when you talk to yourself?

The fascinating thing about our negative self talk is that it creates negative moods. It may seem to you that your bad mood originated out of nowhere: "I just woke up on the wrong side of the bed this morning." Try this the next time you find yourself falling into a funk. Ask yourself, what was I just thinking about? If you catch yourself early enough you will clearly see a direct correlation between your self-defeating, negative, fearful thoughts and your mood.

PAY ATTENTION TO YOUR THOUGHTS

This is important because it becomes so much easier to create a life we want and to tap into our inner wisdom for guidance when we are in a positive and light-hearted mood. When we're happy, we think differently. The world is full of potential, support, and opportunity. Conversely, when we are depressed and down, everything seems hopeless and we feel filled with dread.

Author and speaker, Barbara DeAngelis, describes of the connection between our moods and our self talk, "If your day is full of little mean, dark thoughts, is it any wonder you feel crabby? Maybe it's because you let your mind run wild like a dog putting its nose into garbage everywhere."

I believe that God wants us to live a life of passion, joy, enthusiasm, and love, whatever our circumstances. One of the primary ways we can begin to create that wonderful life is through our beliefs. Begin to act as if you already have the life you want. How would someone who is prosperous believe and act? How would someone who believes they are worthy of love believe and act?

You create your thoughts. Your thoughts create your intentions. Your intentions attract the guidance necessary to cause you to take action. Your actions bring about the results you want to achieve. What kind of life experiences do you want

to attract? Water, fertilize, and nurture those thoughts with great care because the thoughts you hold in your mind now predict your future life.

If you are having trouble replacing your old self talk try this: The next time you are bothered by a nagging, negative thought simply say out loud or to yourself the word, "NEXT!" It will serve as a reminder that you are finished with the old way and that you do not want to create it in your reality any longer. You might even want to get a few close friends involved in your process. If they catch you uttering words that indicate the old negative you is speaking up again, they can yell, "NEXT!"

The next time you find yourself unable to break out of a negative thinking pattern do something to change your state of mind. Take action by doing something that is fun and enjoyable. Get yourself out of the old state of mind as quickly as possible. Penney Peirce, the author of *The Intuitive Way*, put it this way: "I can't do anything about the thoughts that come into my head, but I can do something about the ones that stay there!" Once you get into the habit of doing this you will find that you are able to create the new life you desire and deserve.

SAY "NO" TO NEGATIVITY

When beliefs come up via your self talk, try saying, "Up until now ....." Here is what it would look like:

Your old self talk: "I'll never be successful."
Your new self talk: "I haven't been successful up until now. Now what I want to create is

....

and I believe it's possible."

Your old self talk: "I'll never have enough money."
Your new self talk: "I haven't had enough money up until now.

The new belief I have about money is

....

and I believe it's possible."

"I'VE LEARNED THAT ONE WAY TO BRING MY GREATEST LONGINGS TO THE SURFACE IS TO NOTICE HOW ALIVE THEY MAKE ME FEEL."

MARY MANIN MORRISSEY

THE YEARNINGS OF YOUR SOUL

Babies come into this life knowing what it is they are supposed to do. They are very connected to what brings joy and makes them happy. As they grow older, children begin to bow to external influences, and allow themselves to be talked out of what they love.

MANY OF MY CLIENTS DO THE SAME THING. THEY PUT ASIDE THEIR YEARNINGS. They do what is expected of them, like taking the first job that is offered out of college, and it defines not just their careers, but their whole life. They seem to be afraid that nothing else will show up if they take a chance on their dreams.

Some of the toughest questions I am asked are by people who have put aside their true dreams and aspirations. They feel depressed, enervated, and lacking direction. They ask, "Why am I going through this?" "What am I doing wrong?" or "What can I do to get out of it?" I know that I am expected to come up with some easy answer. "Don't worry, your prince charming is just around the corner." Or "Just go to this alternative physician and she'll fix you right up!"

However, I think the answer to these "dark nights of the soul" is much more complex. You awaken to whom you really are through a process of being in relationship with others, building your careers, making choices, raising your children, and

"ARE YOU BORED WITH LIFE?

THEN THROW YOURSELF

INTO SOME WORK

YOU BELIEVE IN WITH

ALL YOUR HEART,

LIVE FOR IT, DIE FOR IT,

AND YOU WILL FIND

HAPPINESS

THAT YOU HAD THOUGHT COULD

NEVER BE YOURS."

DALE CARNEGIE

dealing with your parents. This is how you learn the lessons you are here to learn. Through a bout with cancer you may have grown in courage. Through dealing with a critically ill parent you may have learned compassion. Through being born with a disability you may have learned persistence. Through going through a difficult divorce you may have learned about forgiveness. As you co-create with God to bring your dream to fruition, you willingly step into the unknown. You expand your view of yourself as you fulfill your potential and ultimately grow into a greater, more compassionate and loving human being.

FOLLOW YOUR INTUITIVE YEARNINGS

When you were a child you probably had a much clearer idea about what made you happy. You were willing to try new things and take risks without too much thought. As you got older you probably felt a lot of restrictions. You might have been told that being an accountant was better than being an actress. Your parents may have told you they would pay for your business degree but not art school.

As an adult you may have gained a practical understanding about those requests. If you heard suggestions like those and heeded them, you probably ended up feeling very out of touch with your true calling. You may have made a practice of overriding your inner messages in search of more pragmatic visions.

What did you want to be when you were a kid? In my neighborhood I was the oldest girl. We lived on a dead end street with a deep forest on one end and fields on either side. I would spend hours with the younger kids playing a game I called "Fairies and Angels." I had an amazing fantasy life, and I would create elaborate stories about angels and fairies helping us out of our imaginary predicaments. We would be in the woods pretending we were in enemy territory and unable to escape. I would whisper, "What do the angels and fairies have to say?" Of course, being the big kid on the block, I never really let any of the others receive messages. I would hear the angel message and off we would go on a new mission! That is how I spent my childhood. Is it any wonder I

> ## "AH, BUT A MAN'S REACH SHOULD EXCEED HIS GRASP, OR WHAT'S A HEAVEN FOR?"
>
> ROBERT BROWNING

ended up becoming a psychic and helping people solve their predicaments through my inner guidance? My whole childhood primed me for this!

Recognizing and following your intuitive yearnings to find your true calling is not an easy process. Following your inner path can be quite challenging and demand a great deal of courage. You can imagine that I did not make an easy transition from a kid who likes to play "angels and fairies" to a life as a successful psychic and writer.

James Allen wrote, "Dream lofty dreams, and as you dream, so shall you become. Your vision is the promise of what you shall one day be; your ideal is the prophecy of what you shall at last unveil." It is a little frightening to pay attention to the yearning of your soul and dream big dreams. What if you fail? What then? Have you had a fantasy about something you wanted to create? Have you put your goals on hold? Let's work at putting those dreams on the front burner again.

EXPAND YOUR COMFORT ZONE

If you can create your dream by yourself, your dream is probably not big enough. Your inner wisdom is your guide who is there to assist you. Your greatest dreams require that you learn to practice new thinking and expand your comfort zone. Oscar Hammerstein said it well, "A dream cannot come true unless you dream that dream."

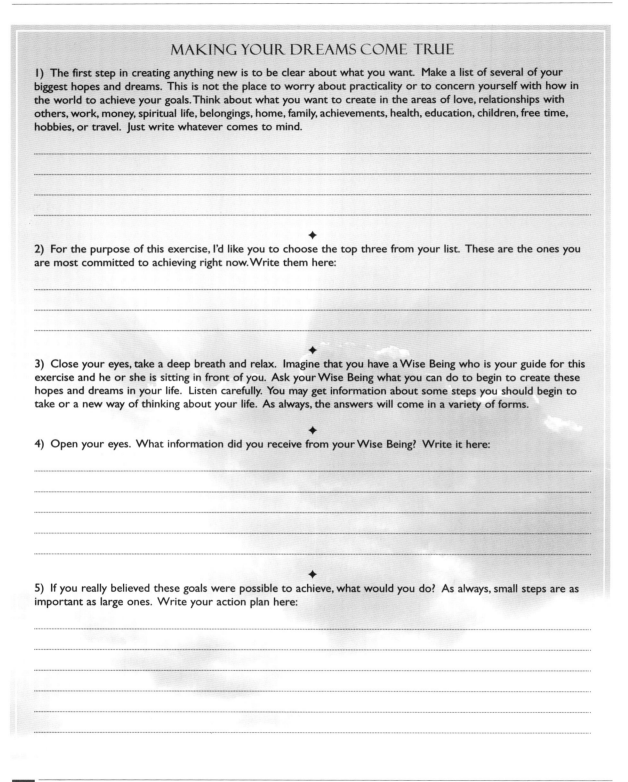

MAKING YOUR DREAMS COME TRUE

1) The first step in creating anything new is to be clear about what you want. Make a list of several of your biggest hopes and dreams. This is not the place to worry about practicality or to concern yourself with how in the world to achieve your goals. Think about what you want to create in the areas of love, relationships with others, work, money, spiritual life, belongings, home, family, achievements, health, education, children, free time, hobbies, or travel. Just write whatever comes to mind.

✦

2) For the purpose of this exercise, I'd like you to choose the top three from your list. These are the ones you are most committed to achieving right now. Write them here:

✦

3) Close your eyes, take a deep breath and relax. Imagine that you have a Wise Being who is your guide for this exercise and he or she is sitting in front of you. Ask your Wise Being what you can do to begin to create these hopes and dreams in your life. Listen carefully. You may get information about some steps you should begin to take or a new way of thinking about your life. As always, the answers will come in a variety of forms.

✦

4) Open your eyes. What information did you receive from your Wise Being? Write it here:

✦

5) If you really believed these goals were possible to achieve, what would you do? As always, small steps are as important as large ones. Write your action plan here:

As you begin to commit to achieving the hopes and dreams on your list, inner messages will pop into your mind to give you inspiration and wise direction. Paying attention is the key to this guidance. It is always there. If you navigate by the map of your intuition, miracles can happen in your life. The directions for how to achieve the yearnings of your soul will begin to appear.

When you start taking small steps towards your dream, you enter a new place, a new paradigm, and begin to see possibilities and solutions that did not seem to be there before. A new world opens up. Thoreau said, "If one advances confidently in the direction of his dreams, he will meet with a success unexpected in common hours."

On your way to creating your new life, you are required to grow and change and to let go of what no longer serves you. Sometimes this is a hard process and one that touches many of your deepest fears. Have courage. Know that you create what you want through a series of ups and downs. When you are in a down cycle, know that you will come up again.

CONTRIBUTE YOUR GIFTS

When I give readings, I often receive information in symbolic images. One of the more common ones is a representation of a big puzzle with a piece missing. When I see that picture in my mind's eye, I know that my client is not doing what he or she is here to do. Each of us brings to this world our own unique gifts, talents, and abilities. We each have a piece of the puzzle that we are here to share with others. If we cast aside our inner guidance that continually informs us of our mission and purpose in life, we are not contributing our gifts. Your uniqueness that makes you who you are. The puzzle will not be whole without the piece you have to offer.

"BEFORE YOU CAN DO SOMETHING THAT YOU'VE NEVER DONE BEFORE, YOU HAVE TO BE ABLE TO IMAGINE IT'S POSSIBLE."

JEAN SHINODA BOLEN

"TRIALS ARE BUT LESSONS THAT YOU FAILED TO LEARN PRESENTED ONCE AGAIN, SO WHERE YOU MADE A FAULTY CHOICE BEFORE, YOU CAN NOW MAKE A BETTER ONE AND THUS ESCAPE ALL PAIN THAT WHAT YOU CHOSE BEFORE HAS BROUGHT TO YOU."

A COURSE IN MIRACLES

FLOWING GRACEFULLY THROUGH CHANGE

Many people come to me when they are going through changes in their lives. This change often starts on an inner level with a feeling — even before there is an outer change. You know you do not like your job any longer and that it is time to leave, but to where and to what and how do you begin? I believe that when you are feeling these seemingly negative feelings, they are simply one of the ways God communicates through your inner wisdom that it's time for a change.

WHEN IT IS TIME FOR A CHANGE IN YOUR LIFE, YOUR WISE INNER BEING has quite a few ways to let you know. The most common way you might experience is that you feel restless, anxious, or bored. When you consistently feel any of these ways, consider it a signal that it is time to let go of something that no longer works. For most of us, discomfort often creates the motivation for change. If you become uncomfortable enough, you eventually take action to leave the job you dislike, or work on a relationship that has been neglected. You do whatever is necessary to move into a better-feeling place.

The dilemma comes for most of us when we allow ourselves to live with the uneasiness we feel. Instead of seeing it as a signal for change, we decide that maybe the discomfort is not so bad and we allow ourselves to stay in the old rut. However, if we ignore the symptoms long enough, our intuition is apt to see that we are not getting the message — and then turn up the volume on the communication it is trying to send. Ignore your discomfort long enough, and it will eventually turn into a crisis.

Before I started giving readings, I thought that everyone knew precisely what they wanted and I was the only one who did not. I seemed to be surrounded by people who knew what they wanted to do or be. One person was clear he wanted to be in sales. Another said that his dream was to make it big in advertising. One friend said that her life's desire was to have kids and be a good parent. Maybe those people stood out because they had clear desires and could articulate them. I was not one of them and I have since found that I have a lot of company.

Many people look at me blankly when I ask them about their hopes and dreams. For most of us there is no connection between what we hope for and dream about and what we actually create in our lives. What I have discovered in giving readings to thousands of clients is that there *is* a direct connection between what happens to you and what thoughts and images you dwell on.

WHEN YOU ARE FACED WITH UNCERTAINTY

What are some of the bigger changes or transitions that affect you?

- ✦ You change jobs.
- ✦ You are down-sized out of your company.
- ✦ You experience ill health.
- ✦ A friend of many years moves away.
- ✦ Your spouse asks for a divorce.
- ✦ Your child leaves for college.
- ✦ Your biggest client goes to the competition.
- ✦ A loved one becomes ill or dies.

Many times in our lives we are faced with uncertainty. What do you do when you reach the end of something? The changes that come about are not necessarily of your choosing, so what is the right way to proceed?

I have a client named Paul. At the time Paul first came to see me he was an industry leader in sales. He came to see me over a period of a few years and began to complain about his work. "Lynn, I hate this work. I have no passion for it any longer. I feel tired and exhausted by the expectations everyone seems to have for me and that I have for myself.

But how can I stop? I'm at the top. People don't quit something they're succeeding at!"

I asked Paul if he was passionate about anything. He lit up as he told me about an idea he had for teaching people what he knew about sales and motivation. We spoke about this at length. I explained that when we take small steps towards something, God will often show us the most direct path to our dreams. At the mention of actually changing his job, Paul looked deflated. "I can't do it," he said, "I make too much money at what I do now. I'd be giving it all up to take that risk. What if I failed?"

Each time Paul came to see me, he complained about his work. People were starting to become envious of his success. Someone had called him to task over a relatively small incident and a big crisis erupted. I told him that I felt each of these situations was a message to at least try something new. It was clear that the passion for his work was no longer fueling him. He was increasingly tired, anxious, and full of fear about his future. He began thinking very negatively about his situation, fearing that he had a colleague who was out to undermine his success.

I pointed out to Paul that he was ignoring his own intuition (and mine). Over the span of the next several months, one crisis after another erupted in his work. Each time he came to see me he was desperate to do something else in his career. Paul was receiving intuitive information that

> **"IF YOU HAVE BUILT CASTLES IN THE AIR, YOUR WORK NEED NOT BE LOST; THAT IS WHERE THEY SHOULD BE. NOW PUT THE FOUNDATIONS UNDER THEM."**
>
> HENRY DAVID THOREAU

> ❝WE ARE MEMBERS OF A VAST COSMIC ORCHESTRA, IN WHICH EACH LIVING INSTRUMENT IS ESSENTIAL TO THE COMPLEMENTARY AND HARMONIOUS PLAYING OF THE WHOLE.❞
>
> J. ALLEN BOONE

TIME FOR A CHANGE

1) Write a few lines about something you feel unhappy about in your life right now:

_____

_____

2) If you could wave a magic wand and create a happy, new situation, what would that be?

_____

_____

3) Make a list of friends, community, and family members that could help you:

_____

_____

4) List some books you can read or classes you can take that could help you:

_____

_____

5) What other resources might you have to help you create a positive change?

_____

_____

6) What steps are you willing to take to access and utilize your resources?

_____

_____

supported his choice to leave his industry and yet he seemed unable to make a move. My perception was that these were "intuitive nudges" he needed to heed. If he didn't, the situation would be taken out of his hands.

The next call I received was from Paul telling me he had been asked to leave his company and possibly even the industry. After several months of turmoil and severe depression, he finally realized that he was being offered an opportunity to create a new life for himself and began the career he dreamed about. Two years passed before I heard from him again. He called to tell me how thrilled he is with the new business he started. His clients love him and he is full of enthusiasm. He told me that he made $90,000 in the last month doing what he loves. He volunteers time each week to talk with men in prison about coping with change from a spiritual perspective. Paul has become a happy man.

DREAM, REFLECT, EXPLORE

Think about taking time over the next few months to dream, explore, and reflect. This might come in the form of journal writing, meditating, or taking a class in a topic that interests you. This may not necessarily be the time to create some new and big goal. But it is a time to figure out what is fun, enjoyable, and energizing.

When you listen to the whispers of your soul and take small steps forward, a new dream emerges. Mary Manin Morrissey said, "As you grow into your dream, your fears grow along with you. Courage is action in the face of fear." Sometimes we just have to be willing to move into some unknown territory and look our fears in the face. That is how our soul challenges us to grow. So, have courage. And be sure to have fun!

"BRING US BACK TO OUR CENTER AND WE WILL RETURN THERE WITH GLADNESS. RENEW US NOW AS YOU HAVE IN DAYS GONE BY."

HEBREW PRAYER

TRUST IN PRAYER

Remember "All In The Family," the wonderful show in the '80s with Archie and Edith Bunker? One of my favorite lines was when Edith asked Archie if he understood what faith is. "Yeah, Edith," blurted Archie, "Faith means believing something that nobody in their right mind would believe." What is prayer? Many people think of it as conversation with God. Others think of prayer as sitting in silence, feeling and experiencing a divine presence which is calming and healing. Whatever your definition, prayer is a powerful vehicle to elicit change, help us with issues of faith, and provide guidance and wisdom.

HOW DO YOU PRAY? IF YOU BEG GOD FOR A SPECIFIC OUTCOME and you do not get it, does it mean God is not listening? Is there a way that works and a way that does not? Is prayer just repeating the words that you learned in religious education class as a child? As far as I know there is not a "Miss Manner's Guide to Correct Prayer," so how do you know if you are doing it right?

TURNING POINTS

Prayer is more than the expectation that God will simply grant our requests if we have enough faith, are good and worthy people, and we pray "correctly." In my opinion, it isn't that easy. You may want to "pray away" an illness that is actually providing you with an opportunity to take the time to rediscover a lost part of yourself. You may have lost your job and pray to get it back, and yet God may be helping you – through the loss of your job – to redirect your life in a new and invigorating way. You might wish that God would wreak vengeance on someone who has betrayed you, but God's plan may be to provide you with a deeper capacity for compassion and forgiveness – through the trauma of betrayal.

Any personal ordeal you face is a turning point. Within any crisis are opportunities and choices. Your personal difficulty provides you with the tools to lead a deeper and richer life if you allow it. To have faith means that you surrender to the wisdom of God, knowing that at the center of every storm is a place of peace and calm. Your challenge in every

> **"GOD BE IN MY HEAD AND IN MY UNDERSTANDING. GOD BE IN MY EYES AND IN MY LOOKING. GOD BE IN MY MOUTH AND IN MY SPEAKING. GOD BE IN MY HEART AND IN MY THINKING. GOD BE AT MY END AND AT MY DEPARTING."**
>
> HYMNS ANCIENT AND MODERN

situation is to find that place. It is not so much to pray for a specific outcome but to know that whatever happens, you will grow in your capacity for peace, cooperation, love, compassion, forgiveness, and healing. I believe this is truly the reason we are all here on the earth.

Dawna Markova writes in her powerful book *No Enemies Within*, "As adults we often fear that which has the greatest capacity to heal us. I believe that real safety lies in your willingness not to run away from yourself. The enemies you face will break you open, so that what needs to come through [for your healing] has a passageway."

I had a client tell me that she can get through times of great turbulence in her life because she trusts those

are times when God is working most powerfully to help her change. Ernest Holmes, the founder of the Science of Mind Church agrees with her: "When the change comes, we should welcome it with a smile on the lips and a song in the heart."

I believe that each thought you think is a form of prayer. You are provided with a strong intellect to choose your goals and visions. You can use your imagination to see the kind of life you want and begin to create it. You have been given the gifts of decisions, intuition, and various individual talents. You can use these gifts to create joy and happiness for yourself and others, or you can ignore these gifts to your detriment. The choice is yours.

The purpose of prayer is to ask for help and guidance from the wisdom that fills, surrounds, and informs our lives and our world. Morris Adler said, "Our prayers are answered not when we are given what we ask, but when we are challenged to be what we can be." Through prayer we come to understand that God is not only there to guide us through the difficulties we face, but also provides the force that brings about our ultimate healing.

So how does all this work on a practical level? When I have a problem or difficulty, I talk to God. This morning part of my prayer went like this, "God, I feel scared about writing this book. I feel overwhelmed and I've got the whole day set aside for writing. What if the words don't come? What if I don't do a good job? Please put your wisdom in my mind and my heart and deliver it to my fingers so I can write what you want people to know."

I followed this with a period of silence. After all,

> **"THE PEACE OF GOD WHICH PASSES ALL UNDERSTANDING."**
>
> THE BOOK OF COMMON PRAYER

> **"TO PRAY OR MEDITATE, I TAKE IMAGES THAT INSPIRE ME. I TAKE SUCH WORDS AS THE 23RD PSALM OR THE LORD'S PRAYER, AND I CALL FORTH MY VISION OF A MASTER SOUL OR AN ANGEL. I WORK WITH LIGHT, DRAWING LIGHT INTO MY BODY AND MAGNIFYING IT."**
>
> ALAN COHEN

I am not the one giving directions (although sometimes I would like to!). I just want to let God know what I am worried and concerned about and then listen intently for an answer. Someone once said, "Prayer is talking to God and meditation is allowing God to answer." I imagine placing my worries into an energy of divine love and wisdom. The answers return to me through that same energy in the vehicle of my intuition.

FINDING PEACE IN PRAYER

What I received from my prayer this morning was a sense of peace. I sat down at my computer and thought, "Okay. I can do this." The fear lessened, the words came, and I felt good about what I wrote. It is often just that simple. A shift in attitude, a position of allowing peace, or a sense of willingness to surrender is all that is needed. Many times the issues I pray about are much deeper, but they still require the same openness to receive guidance in whatever form it comes.

Meditation is often difficult for me. My intention each time I sit down to meditate is to quiet my mind for a few moments and feel God's presence. I try to focus on my breath, but my thoughts hurl themselves around in my brain and I feel like I am trying to herd a bunch of cats. (Don't ever attempt it!) When I find my mind wandering to my to-do list or to the groceries I need to pick up for dinner, I gently bring my thoughts back to God.

If you grew up with the idea of God as a bearded old man judging you from his throne in heaven, the thought of praying and asking for wisdom and peace may be a bit difficult. Try to imagine a new image of God, one that makes you feel understood and loved. Some people experience God as an energy, a feeling, a woman, a spirit, or even as an image of a person they once knew and loved. Talk to the God that feels wise and loving, and share your concerns. Know that you are being listened to by a divine intelligence that is there to help you find your way. You are not alone or abandoned.

One of my favorite quotes on prayer that demonstrates this concept is from author and speaker John Harrichan, who says, "Whenever I feel the world closing in on me, I go to a quiet place that lies somewhere in my soul. I do not reason, analyze, or think. Those will come later. I simply go. And as a frightened child finds comfort and strength in a loving parent, I find my God there. From this place of power, I gather strength to stand firm in the face of fire, to be calm in the midst of thunder. When I emerge from this sanctuary, the world has not changed, but I have. And in my changing, a whole new world is born."

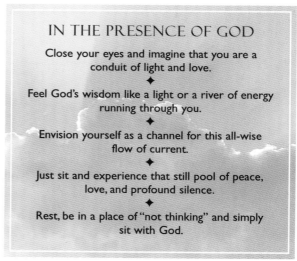

IN THE PRESENCE OF GOD

Close your eyes and imagine that you are a conduit of light and love.

◆

Feel God's wisdom like a light or a river of energy running through you.

◆

Envision yourself as a channel for this all-wise flow of current.

◆

Just sit and experience that still pool of peace, love, and profound silence.

◆

Rest, be in a place of "not thinking" and simply sit with God.

"I LET GO OF HURRY, ANXIETY, PRESSURE, AND WORRY. I CHOOSE PEACE, JOY, RELAXATION, AND RENEWAL. I AM GUIDED IN HOW TO BEST USE MY TIME. I ACCOMPLISH EVERYTHING I AM HERE TO DO AND I HAVE TIME TO ENJOY LIFE RIGHT HERE AND RIGHT NOW."

REVEREND DONALD WELSH

CHOOSING JOY

Those who enjoy the greatest happiness are not extraordinary people. They are not necessarily the wealthiest or the most well-known. Those who sparkle with joy are most often ordinary people who have not lost their sense of wonder. They find a gift in each moment of living. They enjoy the few moments of pleasantries with their neighbor; they marvel at the dew glistening on a flower petal; they take delight in a child's giggles. They find a gift in each moment of their life.

I THINK ONE OF THE BIGGEST MISCONCEPTIONS MOST OF US HAVE IN THIS LIFE is that something has to change in order for us to be happy. Don't get me wrong. I find it much easier to be happy when I have enough money, good health, great friends, and meaningful work. One of my first clients, a young man I will call Dan, was in his early thirties when he came to see me. I remember that he sat down opposite me and in a very business-like manner took out a list of questions that he had typed up and wanted to ask me. His first question was:

"When will I be happy?"

At first I thought he was joking. I remember wondering if Dan thought that it was pre-ordained that on a certain date, say September 11, the quality of happiness was going to be bestowed on him. Maybe he imagined it would be handed out like a diploma. When it became clear that he was serious about his question, I did not know how to respond, so I asked him to explain what he meant.

He said, "I thought that once I got out of high school and away from my family, I'd be happy. Then I thought that once I graduated from college, for sure I'd be happy then. When I got my first job and was finally on my way professionally, I was sure that I'd made it and happiness would be mine. I kept expecting that I'd be happy after getting married, being promoted and getting a big raise, to having my first child. I'm still not happy." He looked at me expectantly. I looked back at him and taking the risk of sounding like a Hallmark card I said, "Did it ever occur to you that you're as happy as you make up your mind to be?"

Who comes to your mind when you think of someone in your life who is happy or content? Frequently, they are very ordinary people. My mother-in-law leaps to mind when I think of someone who is happy. She is a living example of choosing happiness. In fact, her nickname is "Rosie"

> ❝I CANNOT BELIEVE THAT THE INSCRUTABLE UNIVERSE TURNS ON AN AXIS OF SUFFERING; SURELY THE STRANGE BEAUTY OF THE WORLD MUST SOMEWHERE REST ON PURE JOY.❞
>
> LOUISE BOGAN

because of her wonderful disposition. Let me share two viewpoints about her:

1)   Mom is over eighty years old and in failing health. She has macular degeneration causing her to rapidly lose her eyesight; she broke a leg a couple of years ago and has had difficulty walking; and she has recently had to give up driving her beloved old Chevy because of her poor sight. When she was forty, her husband, Bud, died in a car accident; she became a widow with five children to raise. She lost the family home about thirty years ago and now lives in a tiny two-room apartment and has to rely on others for transportation. She lives on a small amount of social security income. All indications suggest that she would be a good candidate for depression.

2)   Here is a recent conversation I had with Mom: "I am so glad to be alive! Isn't it a great day? I just love sitting outside on the lawn and listening to the birds sing. I just sit there and think of all the things I'm grateful for. I think about it every day when I get up and before I go to bed. I pray every day for those people who don't have as much as I do. I have all my kids and grand kids living around me, and I feel so filled up with gratitude. I've lived a long time and God may take me any time, but I'm just going to appreciate every moment I have left."

My mother-in-law is someone who clearly

chooses happiness — and happiness has clearly chosen her. She focuses on all that she has to be grateful for and attracts more of its richness into her life.

Who comes to your mind when you think of someone who is happy? They are probably not the wealthiest or the most famous people you know. Those who sparkle with aliveness are ordinary people like you and me. Like my mother-in-law, they have not lost their wonder of the moment. They cherish the call from a friend. They delight at hearing a child laugh. They have moments in each day when they stop and take a deep breath and simply appreciate the moment. They listen to the breeze blowing through the trees, observe a bird flying, listen to their cat purr. They find a gift in each simple moment of living.

I have found over and over again in working with clients that you attract into your life what you focus on. You can see the results of your dominant thoughts by what is in your life right now. Please understand that this does not happen overnight. You do not simply imagine, "I'd like a million bucks" and find it on your doorstep the next day. Nor do you say, "Gee, I don't feel well" and wake up the next morning with a diagnosis of terminal cancer.

Do you measure your success in life by how much you have achieved, the amount of money you have accumulated, or the possessions you own? You might have seen the bumper sticker, "He who dies with the most toys wins." Life is meant to be enjoyable and rewarding, yet many of us act as if doing all the things society tells us we should will guarantee our rewards at some future point in life.

CHOOSING JOY

William Feather wrote, "No man is a failure who is enjoying life." Your inner guidance unerringly leads you to a life of purpose and fulfillment. Your task is to take the small steps first. It happens over time when you learn to savor the small, seemingly inconsequential moments in life.

Begin to make decisions based on what makes you happy, peaceful, and joyful. This is one of the ways to honor your inner guidance. Your intuition always steers you in the right direction.

Talk show host Oprah Winfrey suggests her viewers keep a "gratitude journal." She writes in hers every night, listing five things she is grateful for from that day. She believes this activity helps connect her with spiritual truth and draws to her even more experiences by which she feels blessed.

Why not try a "Joy Journal?" It works on the same principal, and it is a terrific way to help you pay attention to your inner guidance. What you love to do, what you feel joyful and passionate about – these feelings offer a sign from your Higher Self about what you are meant to do. The poet Rumi wrote, "Let yourself be silently drawn by the strange pull of what you really love. It will not lead you astray."

It is possible to create a life you love, one that is filled with enthusiasm, love, and abundance. Your present life circumstances may seem far removed from that statement, and yet I assure you that if you commit to making decisions from the standpoint of joy, you will begin to live a life that is richly blessed. Author Richard Bach writes, "In the path of your happiness shall you find the learning for which you have chosen this lifetime." Discovering what you love to do is hearing a clarion call from God indicating the direction you are to follow. Have courage, take small steps, keep taking them, and before you know it, you will be living in the "joy flow."

> ❝WE CALL 'HAPPINESS' A CERTAIN SET OF CIRCUMSTANCES THAT MAKES JOY POSSIBLE. BUT WE CALL JOY THAT STATE OF MIND AND EMOTIONS THAT NEEDS NOTHING TO FEEL HAPPY.❞
>
> ANDRÉ GIDE

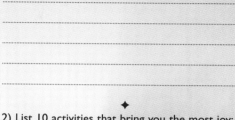

WHAT BRINGS YOU JOY?

1) Think over the past year. What brought you the most joy?

....

....

....

....

....

....

✦

2) List 10 activities that bring you the most joy:

....

....

....

....

....

....

....

....

....

✦

3) Go back to your list in #2 above and write a date next to each activity to indicate the last time you did this.

✦

4) What steps are you willing to take in order to bring these activities into your life on a regular basis?

....

....

....

....

....

"YOU WILL NOT SUDDENLY DEVELOP WEALTH CONSCIOUSNESS IF AND WHEN YOU BECOME 'WEALTHY.' IT'S THE OTHER WAY AROUND. YOU DEVELOP WEALTH CONSCIOUSNESS BY ELIMINATING WORRY, BY TRUSTING IN THE UNIVERSE AND IN YOUR OWN INNER RESOURCES. ONCE YOU SECURE YOUR WEALTH CONSCIOUSNESS, TRUE ABUNDANCE IS JUST AROUND THE CORNER."

RICHARD CARLSON

GOD'S PAYROLL

Of all the issues that people come to me with, money — and the lack of it — is often the most charged. Here is my definition of prosperity: To have the resources necessary to create the life you want and to trust that this will continue. When you have a belief and knowledge that there is abundance in the world, you begin to feel a sense of security. You are able to move towards your dream trusting your inner guidance and knowing that the money or life circumstances you need will be there. Notice I didn't state my definition as "To have a million dollars" (or any other amount). The reason for this is that until you can live your life KNOWING that abundance is your birthright and TRUSTING that it will be there, you will feel poor.

PROSPERITY DOES NOT HAVE TO DO WITH THE *AMOUNT* OF MONEY YOU HAVE. Over and over I have observed that a lack of worry precedes an abundance of success. It is not the other way around!

Some of the poorest people I have ever met have been the wealthiest by anyone else's standards. I have a client named Debbie who has a large inheritance from her family. She does not have to work and can live a fairly luxuriously for the rest of her life. You would think that Debbie would feel wealthy. She does not. In fact, Debbie constantly worries about money. "Have I invested it properly?" "Will I lose the money?" "What is the stock market going to do?" "What do people who know I have money think of me?" If you use my definition of prosperity, Debbie is poor.

DEVELOPING ABUNDANCE CONSCIOUSNESS

I am willing to wager that many of you are making at least twice as much money as you did a decade ago. If you are, ask yourself a simple question, "Am I worrying about money half as much?" If the answer is "No," then making even more money is not going to relieve your worry and anxiety, is it? Here is the honest truth: unless you learn to be happy with what you have, you will not be happy with more.

Prosperity is so much more than a specific dollar amount. When you have a belief and knowledge that abundance is in the world, you begin to feel a

"THERE IS NO SEPARATION BETWEEN US AND GOD – WE ARE DIVINE EXPRESSIONS OF THE CREATIVE PRINCIPLE... THERE CAN BE NO REAL LACK OR SCARCITY; THERE IS NOTHING WE HAVE TO TRY TO ACHIEVE OR ATTRACT; WE CONTAIN THE POTENTIAL FOR EVERYTHING WITH US."

SHAKTI GAWAIN

"IF YOU WANT TO FEEL RICH, JUST COUNT ALL OF THE THINGS YOU HAVE THAT MONEY CAN'T BUY."

ANONYMOUS

sense of security. You will be able to move towards your dream trusting your inner guidance and knowing that the money or life circumstances you need will be there.

Last summer I received a call from a literary agent who proposed I write what became my book, *The Complete Idiot's Guide to Being Psychic*, I was a bit concerned about money. Writing that book on a tight deadline meant that I would have to see fewer clients. Doing intuitive readings was my main source of income.

I meditated about taking the assignment and got a clear "go ahead" from my inner guidance system. I told the agent I would do it and sat back to trust that something would happen to bring in money through some other means. The very afternoon I said "Yes" to the book, my husband called to say that he had received a large contract that provided us with enough money to more than make up for my diminished income.

Now I have to say that God does not act that swiftly all the time! But what I've learned in looking back on my life is that something always works out. I believe that we are all on God's Payroll. When we do our job, which is to follow our inner guidance, we are living the job description that we co-created with God. We get paid when we are doing what we love.

THINKING ABUNDANTLY

The trick is to not get attached to the form in which this income appears. It may come through a part time job to help you pay your bills while you start your new company, or from being laid off from your old job and receiving unemployment insurance that allows you enough time and money

to make a career change and a bigger salary. Once when I was bemoaning the fact that I did not have enough money to buy new clothes, a friend called to say she was moving to Florida and would not need her winter wardrobe. I inherited a closet full of expensive designer clothes in my exact size! God works in mysterious — and sometimes fashionable — ways!

The fact is that you are creating your experience of abundance at every moment. Here is the confusing part: you have either an abundance of scarcity or an abundance of prosperity. If you accept the notion that you create your life through the thoughts and beliefs you hold, then it stands to reason that you continue on the same path until you change it. You need to change your thinking in order to change your life. Have you noticed that you tend to create, over and over again, the same unwanted experiences? You may find different players and slightly differing circumstances, but the outcome is much the same. But remember that you can change your thoughts and thus alter your experiences.

YOUR PROSPERITY GUIDE

What would your life look like if you had all that you wanted? Sometimes in the midst of struggling with what you *do not* want in life, you forget to ask this question. Many people believe that their financial life is fated: "I was born poor so I'll stay poor." Others take a slightly more "new age" approach to explain their current lack of abundance: "I misused money and power in a past life so I'm poor in this one." Other people believe: "My spiritual life is very important; I can't be spiritual and have money."

What would you do if I told you that you have a "Prosperity Guide" inside you, its sole purpose to help you lead a happy, prosperous, and abundant life? Would you believe you deserve such a guide? Would you listen to it if it continually gave you information and direction, or would you tell me all the reasons this guide could not exist or why it could not work for you?

You do have an "Inner Prosperity Guide." It is your intuition. When you begin to pay attention to what your intuition is telling you it will consistently lead you to the only truth it knows, "Abundance is your birthright." It may guide you to new work, the right contacts for your business, a great idea for an invention, or a book to read that opens a door to greater abundance.

I believe that our world is naturally abundant. The Bible states, "Ask and it shall be given to you. Seek and you shall find." When you are doing work you love, you experience no separation between your work and your life. What you love to do and feel guided to do is your life's work. I am aware that this sounds overly simplistic, and perhaps it is. It has taken me years of working with this principle to slowly but surely absorb it and see it work consistently in my life. I found that I had to be diligent about working through old beliefs that did not support this outlook on life.

Making any change in your life often feels uncomfortable at first. You may find that negative thoughts and feelings come to the surface. When I first started working with prosperity principles, I began to feel unworthy. I did not think that I deserved to have money. I observed all the ways that I thought spending money on anything but basic needs was bordering on sinful.

YOUR PASSION = YOUR PROSPERITY

If there is such a thing as a "Prosperity Magnet," I was the opposite. I was working for a non-profit, adult education organization, making little more than what was minimum wage at the time. I held a very deep belief that I was not worthy of any money beyond my basic needs. This belief was clearly manifesting in my life. I used to joke that my car always knew when I had saved $100; it would break down the moment there was any "extra" money in my pocket!

If you find you have pessimistic or negative beliefs about money ask yourself, "What's another way of thinking about this?" or "What do I want to create in my life?" It is important to pay attention to your thoughts. Listen to what you tell yourself about your life situation. Pay special attention to your beliefs about money.

Understand that life has ebbs and flows. Life does not always go in a straight line, even when you are doing everything "right." These new beliefs and outcomes that you are trying to create do not just change things overnight. It would be wonderful to be able to say, "I get it! I've changed; I now believe I can be spiritual and have money" – and have money flow into your life in abundance the next day. Patience is needed here. Just as nature has seasons, cycles, ebbs, and flows, so does your life. Learn to recognize and optimize them.

Pay attention to what you feel passionate about. What is fun for you? What excites you? These are some of the ways your intuition informs you about your life's purpse and directs you toward abundance. At first do not overwhelm yourself by trying to figure out how to make a living out of it. I have found that when you taking steps in the direction of your passion, God opens doors you never imagined were there.

"IT IS NOT HOW MUCH WE HAVE, BUT HOW MUCH WE ENJOY, THAT MAKES HAPPINESS."

CHARLES HADDON SPURGEON

HOW DO YOU THINK ABOUT MONEY?

1) Is there a problem area in your financial life? If so, describe it here.

_____

_____

_____

_____

✦

2) What beliefs do you hold about money? Do you believe that there is never enough? Perhaps you think that other people can be rich but you never will. Whatever your beliefs, describe a few of them here.

_____

_____

_____

_____

_____

✦

3) Sit quietly and envision what you would like to create instead. Imagine paying your bills easily, and having enough money left over to invest wisely. See yourself having fun and contributing to worthy causes. Fill your visualization with as much positive emotion as you can. Envision yourself enjoying having money.

✦

4) Ask your inner guidance this question, "What could I do to experience this abundance in my life?" Listen quietly for the answer.

✦

5) Write about the feelings, impressions, knowledge, and words you receive.

_____

_____

_____

_____

_____

_____

_____

_____

_____

_____

_____

"THERE'S NO USE TRYING," ALICE SAID, "ONE CAN'T BELIEVE IMPOSSIBLE THINGS." "I DARE SAY YOU HAVEN'T HAD MUCH PRACTICE," SAID THE QUEEN, "WHEN I WAS YOUR AGE, I ALWAYS DID IT FOR HALF-AN-HOUR A DAY. WHY SOMETIMES I'VE BELIEVED AS MANY AS SIX IMPOSSIBLE THINGS BEFORE BREAKFAST."

LEWIS CARROLL

WHAT WOULD YOU DO IF YOU KNEW YOU WOULDN'T FAIL?

What if you knew for certain that everything you are presently worried about would work out okay, that you had the inner wisdom to handle anything life presents, that even if something difficult came your way, you would still be okay?

WHAT IF YOU HAD A CONSTANT SOURCE OF ABUNDANCE FLOWING TO YOU at all times? What if there really was a divine plan for your life? If you did not have to worry, what would you do?

I have a friend who is a career counselor. One of her favorite questions for her clients is, "What would you do if you knew you wouldn't fail?" So many of us get stuck in that phase where we do not take any steps forward because we are afraid that what we want most won't happen.

In my sessions with clients, I am often surprised at the number of people who throw in the towel and give up on their dream right before it is going to happen.

What if you knew for certain that everything you are presently worried about would work out? What if you knew that you had the inner wisdom to handle any life situation that came along? What if you knew that even if something difficult came your way, you would still be okay? What if you knew that

"FINISH EACH DAY AND BE DONE WITH IT. YOU HAVE DONE WHAT YOU COULD. SOME BLUNDERS AND ABSURDITIES NO DOUBT CREPT IN; FORGET THEM AS SOON AS YOU CAN. TOMORROW IS A NEW DAY; BEGIN IT WELL AND SERENELY AND WITH TOO HIGH A SPIRIT TO BE ENCUMBERED WITH YOUR OLD NONSENSE."

RALPH WALDO EMERSON

you had a constant source of abundance flowing to you at all times? What if you did not have to worry? What would you do?

In the 25 years I have been giving readings, one of the saddest comments I hear is "I'd love to (fill in the blank) but I know it wouldn't work." But what if you knew that you were guaranteed success? What if I could gaze into my crystal ball and tell you that if you began to take small steps towards what you love and kept walking you would be happy, creative, and successful? Well, I am telling you. Over and over I see those baby steps we all need to take as being a huge key to our eventual success. It is as if you are telling God, "Okay. I trust the guidance you're giving me and I'm willing to trust it enough to take action."

WHEN THINGS DO NOT WORK OUT

I remember a poster from my youth that said something like, "Stress is doing the same thing over and over and expecting a different outcome." Do you find yourself trying to make a decision and then rehearsing in your mind all the horrible outcomes that could occur? When using your inner guidance, it helps to be clear about the outcome you want. Many people get stuck in the process by thinking of all the things they do not want. When you are clear about your goals, your intuition can inform you about the clearest, most direct path to achieve it.

God often puts situations in our paths that may not be what we want, but may be just what we need. For example, during my twenties I had worked almost exclusively for non-profit organizations, which also meant I was working for a non-profit salary: I was barely making ends meet. I decided that I wanted to make more money but still work for an organization that provided a service that I believed in. I prayed a lot about what I could do next. A few months later I received a call offering me a job as an operations manager working for a socially responsible venture capital fund. I leapt at the opportunity, seeing this as the answer to my prayers even though it meant moving out of the Boston area and away from my friends to upstate New York.

"THERE ARE NO SHORTCUTS TO ANYPLACE WORTH GOING.

BEVERLY SILLS

To make a long story short, once I moved there the job fell through. The fund never really got off the ground in the way the people who were running it thought it would. They certainly did not need a manager, and thus I was out of a job. I was devastated. I had moved everything I owned to New York, had very little money, no job or job prospects, and very few contacts in the area that would help me create new work for myself. The worst part was that I felt abandoned by God. I could not figure out why I had felt so guided to this job only to have it collapse as soon as I started. Everything about this decision felt right, and I truly felt guided to take it. This hit at a core belief I had about how life worked: "If I followed my inner guidance everything would work out."

HELP FROM UNEXPECTED PLACES

I felt quite adrift and depressed. I made some attempts to find some other work over the next several weeks, looking in the newspaper and calling head hunters. I was beginning to feel very scared and abandoned by God. I remember one night trying to pray and listen for what to do next and ended up yelling at God for leading me in this obviously wrong direction.

Shortly after this I met a woman named Megan. She was a friend of a friend, and I had given her an informal psychic reading after dinner at the friend's house one evening. Although she did not show it at the time, she felt profoundly affected by what I had said in our brief session. She began to refer her friends to me for readings. Before I knew it, her friends were referring their friends and I had a part time psychic reading business that enabled me to support myself.

GOD'S PLAN

As I look back on all this with fifteen years' hindsight, I can see clearly that God had a plan for me. During that time when the job fell through, I learned a lot even though I didn't understand it at the time. I did not get what I wanted but I got what I needed. I learned to have patience. I learned I could make a living through readings, something I am sure I never would have tried if I had not been "forced" to. Most important, I learned I had courage and I learned about taking risks.

What is your dream? What would you do if you knew you would not fail? The purpose of the exercise in this chapter is to help you answer those questions. Most of us do not dream big enough. This is not the place to figure out how you are going to create what you want. It is the place to imagine it. Be willing to have fun with it. Try different scenarios. If what you choose at first does not feel right, change it! This exercise is best done on large sheets of paper with magic markers, paints, colored pencils, and crayons. If drawing or painting is not your thing, get out a stack of old magazines and cut out pictures of what you want to create. In each of the following areas write, draw, or paste images and words about your dreams and passions. You want to fully imagine what it would look and feel like if you could create the successful and abundant life you deserve. Don't hold yourself back by what you think is possible. Go for it!

In order to make your dream come true, start to think of doing something simple. This could be anything that makes you feel good. Those small things are part of your amazing inner guidance system. Step by step, take action on what feels energizing, fun, and relaxing. Congratulations! You are on the path to using your gift of intuition to create the life you want.

"YET THIS IDEA OF SUBMISSION TO DEEP INTUITION APPEARS TO BE EXACTLY WHAT MANY SUCCESSFUL PEOPLE IN A WIDE VARIETY OF FIELDS HAVE COME TO ADOPT."

WILLIS HARMAN

ENVISIONING YOUR IDEAL LIFE

The overall vision that I have for my life is:

....

The details of what I would like to create include:
Home:

....

Travel:

....

Relationship(s):

....

Work/Career:

....

Possessions:

....

Service to others:

....

Other area(s) of your choosing:

....

....

How do you feel now that you have begun the process? Look back over what you have created. What are the one or two things that you are most excited about? Write them here:

....

....

Many people find it helpful to visualize their intuition coming to them in the form of a guide or wise being. Close your eyes and imagine that in front of you. A loving and wise being sits in front of you. Feel yourself being filled and surrounded by love and compassion. (pause) Tell this wise one what you would like to create in your life. (pause). Ask your guide, "What do I need to do in order to begin to make my dream come true?" Receive the answer in whatever form it comes. (pause)
Open your eyes. What action step will you do within the next week that can take you closer to your goal?

....

....

....

"THERE IS A VITALITY, A LIFE FORCE, AN ENERGY, A QUICKENING THAT IS TRANSLATED THROUGH YOU INTO ACTION, AND BECAUSE THERE IS ONLY ONE OF YOU IN ALL OF TIME, THIS EXPRESSION IS UNIQUE. AND IF YOU BLOCK IT, IT WILL NEVER EXIST THROUGH ANY OTHER MEDIUM AND BE LOST."

MARTHA GRAHAM

WHEN IT'S TIME TO TAKE ACTION

One of the principles in creating a life you love is to "act as if." What would your life look like if you acted as if you were:

- *sure of yourself?*
- *filled with creative ideas?*
- *an extrovert?*
- *well liked?*
- *destined to succeed?*
- *full of energy?*
- *happy and purposeful?*

WHEN YOU BELIEVE THAT YOU HAVE THE QUALITIES YOU NEED in order to have a successful life, you begin to draw new experiences to you. Your intuitive guidance provides you with information about going in the new direction you have chosen.

Taking action is the part that is most often left out of the current information on creative visualization and the use of affirmations. For many people, action is the most difficult part of creating the life they want.

TAKE A LEAP OF FAITH

The Buddha said, "There are only two mistakes one can make along the road to truth: not going all the way, and not starting." You may need to get a better job. You may feel guided to begin a new business. Your intuition may tell you it is time for a move to a new location with better opportunities. People often experience a great deal of uncertainty and fear in this part of the process because it means leaving behind what is known and safe. What you have may not be

> **"KNOWING IS NOT ENOUGH. RISK KNOWLEDGE WITH ACTION AND THEN YOU WILL KNOW WHETHER IT IS GENUINE, PRETENSION, OR JUST INFORMATION."**
>
> SRI GURUDEV CHITRABHANU

what you want, but it is something that you know.

Nevertheless, in order to create more of what you want, you have to take a leap into the unknown. Such a transition often evokes our deepest fears, our oldest wounds. So this is a time to be gentle with yourself, to treat yourself with loving kindness. Talk to yourself as you would to your best friend if he or she were going through this change. Speak to yourself gently and trust your own pace and rhythm. Listen to your guidance and take action based on its wisdom. If you are not sure what your guidance is saying, keep asking and take small, slow steps. Be patient. Change often takes time.

BUILDING BRIDGES

People usually come for a consultation when they have a decision to make. I have found a common assumption that everyone else is 100% sure and certain of their decisions and that they make them easily and effortlessly. This is the farthest thing from the truth! Most of us are filled with angst; we vacillate when we try to make a decision. The more life-changing the potential decision, the more we waver. I have what I call the 60/40 rule: if I feel slightly more certain than not that the decision I am about to make is a good one, I go for it.

One of my clients, whom I will call Pete, saw me first about a year ago. He had a stress-filled, demanding job with an accounting company that required an 80-hour-a-week commitment. By his telling, this was a "good job." Yet he constantly felt tired and irritable and had no time for his friends and family, or for relaxing. In other words, he had no balance in his life. The next time he came to see me he had decided to leave his job, yet he was wracked with indecision. "What if I can't find a new job? Maybe I should stay at this job another year. I work for a prestigious company. I must be crazy to think of leaving."

Pete and I talked about his desire to have more balance in his life and his ultimate goal to work for a sports team as a CFO. In his present job he had no possibility of either of those things happening. He felt locked in and afraid to take a leap of faith because there was no "safety net" to catch him.

Most people feel they need a guarantee that things will work out or they are afraid to make a move. I am in favor of what I call "building bridges" instead of "leaps of faith." When there is a bridge, you have a slightly better chance of not falling into the rocks when you try to change your location! Building a bridge requires taking a few small steps toward what you think you want.

It does not necessarily involve a big risk such as leaving a job or ending a relationship. It could be as simple as taking a class in something you are interested in or doing some volunteer work for an organization you may want to work for. What I find is that when you take the small steps to build the bridge, God opens doors for you that you may not have seen before. Opportunities arise and

> **"DO THE THING AND YOU WILL HAVE THE POWER."**
>
> RALPH WALDO EMERSON

> **"COMMITMENT LEADS TO ACTION AND ACTION BRINGS YOUR DREAM CLOSER."**

MARCIA WIEDER

synchronicities begin to occur.

I asked Pete, "What small step could you take that would lead you in the direction of your dreams?" He thought for awhile and said that he had always wanted to live in Arizona where he had been to school and still had a lot of friends. Maybe he could take a vacation there and apply for jobs and do a bit of networking. We agreed that would be a terrific plan because it combined a much needed vacation with a step in the right direction to further his career goals.

When I later heard from Pete, he told me he had found a new job in Arizona. He had met with one of his friends from school who had some athletic team connections and helped him get a job as a comptroller for a baseball league. He had found what he wanted by taking just one step!

THE POWER OF SMALL STEPS

This exercise offers some examples of small steps you might take to create the life you want. Notice that none of them require you to make an immediate decision about a life change or to take a big risk. All you are doing is information gathering, or, as I call it, "putting energy out there."

George Bernard Shaw said, "People are always blaming their circumstances for what they are. I don't believe in circumstances. The people who get on in this world are people who get up and look for the circumstances they want and, if they can't find them, make them." Your job is to get clear about your intentions to trust God to open the right doors and to take action when the time is right. Your feelings, hunches, and flashes of insight will signal what actions to take. Your willingness to be spontaneous, follow your inner urges, listen to strong feelings, and act

them will lead you to your goals.

If your thoughts tend to be negative or pessimistic ask yourself, "What's another way of thinking about this?" or "What do I want to create in my life?" Apply "turnarounds" as needed. Remember: would you rather be right or would you rather be happy? Do your beliefs and dominant thoughts express the true expectations you have for your life? As Will Rogers said, "Even if you're on the right track, you'll get run over if you just sit there."

STEP CLOSER TO YOUR DREAMS

Examples:

1) Call a career counselor and make an appointment to discuss your interests. Work with him/her to create an action plan to bring your dreams into reality.

◆

2) Talk to someone who made a successful career change about how they got there.

◆

3) Interview someone who has your dream job.

◆

4) Sign up for a class in something that is either pure fun or a subject you may want to explore for a new career.

◆

5) If you are thinking about a geographic move, go to that place on vacation, subscribe to the local paper, and ask friends for referrals to people living in the area.

◆

6) Research your interests on the Internet or at the library. Small steps count! You are building a bridge to the life you want!!

◆

7) Make an appointment with a financial planner to evaluate how you could make a career switch and at the same time maintain your financial security.

◆

Take action on at least three things each week that move you closer to your goals/visions/ dreams. Making change in your life often feels uncomfortable at first. Small steps count. Put the energy to create new things in your life out into the world. Your intuition will guide you as to what actions to take. The path towards your goal will begin to open up.

"LIFE IS A TEST. IT IS ONLY A TEST. HAD THIS BEEN A REAL LIFE YOU WOULD HAVE BEEN INSTRUCTED WHERE TO GO AND WHAT TO DO."

FROM A POPULAR POSTER

GOD'S LESSON PLAN

When I look back on my life I can see that all of what has transpired thus far has prepared me for exactly what I am doing now. From the vantage point of being in my mid-forties I can peer into my past and see that the crazy job I had at the computer start-up business in my twenties helped me become successful in running my own business. The job I had in college working with disadvantaged kids has added to my understanding of family dynamics, psychology, and motivation. It also added immeasurably to my being able to experience compassion and love for others who are different from me. Even the few months I spent caring for a four-year-old child with Down's Syndrome gave me more patience and the ability to see life from a different perspective.

THROUGH ALL THIS TIME I FELT AS IF I WAS BEING GUIDED BY AN OUTSIDE FORCE and moved along my path. Each experience seems, in retrospect, divinely guided to help me play a particular role in this life. When I realize this, I am filled with wonder. Now when I go through difficult times, I am able to distance myself from the turmoil – to stop and reflect on what new skill, quality, or piece of wisdom I may be learning through this event. This way of thinking about life's changes and challenges has, at times, brought me a measure of peace, often when it is sorely needed.

YOUR DIVINE INSTRUCTION PLAN

When you came to earth you were presented with a specific set of circumstances. Many variables exist: the parents you were born to, whether you experience love or the lack of it, whether your family has an abundance of money or none at all, whether you are sick or healthy. You entered the school of life and whatever your particulars, you have learned to make the most of what you have.

The specific course of instruction in this life's school varies for each of us. Some of you may learn your school lessons through a difficult family situation; others may learn through an ongoing health crisis, death of a loved one, a divorce, or perhaps a financial setback. The instruction plan is divinely guided and is carried in your soul. You have access to it through your intuition.

"NO SOUL THAT ASPIRES CAN EVER FAIL TO RISE; NO HEART THAT LOVES CAN EVER BE ABANDONED. DIFFICULTIES EXIST ONLY THAT IN OVERCOMING THEM WE MAY GROW STRONG."

ANNIE BESANT

I am going to share something of vital importance with you: there will never be a more perfect time to embark your true calling than now. Why should you take this risk? When you follow your heart and begin to take steps towards what you feel truly passionate about, you will have begun the process that brings about an abundant and joyful life, which is what living life intuitively is all about. The biggest error most of us make is waiting for life to be perfect before we begin to make a change.

YOUR INTUITIVE HEART

I am practical enough to understand that most of us have mortgages to pay, groceries to buy, and kids to put through college. I am not suggesting you just chuck your job and think that overnight things will change so dramatically that you will do what you love and the money will follow. However, what would your life look like if you simply started the process towards doing what you love?

What would you like to create in your life? How many of the following are true for you?

+ I look forward to each day with excitement because I love what I do.

+ I have enough abundance to pay my bills, give money to worthy causes, and save and invest for a comfortable retirement.

+ I have balance in my life and time for myself, friends, and family.

+ I feel motivated and productive in my work.

+ I feel loved and appreciated.

+ I feel that the work I do is of service to others.

+ I have more than enough energy to accomplish my tasks as I go about my day.

If you agreed with most of these items, then – congratulations, you are living a life you love! If you have left many or all of them unchecked, you may feel overwhelmed and discouraged. How do you begin to create the change you desire? I have good news for you. By simply being aware of what

you want to create, even in an abstract form, you have begun to attract it to yourself. When you keep your thoughts and heart focused on abundance, friends, community, and support instead of the opposite, you have embarked on a new path.

Your intuition guides you to the right choices through your heart. When you have a choice to make, choose what you are drawn to and feel excited about. Take the action your heart is leading you to. If you catch yourself saying "I have to" or "I should do this or that," take it as a signal from your intuition that you need to refocus on where the positive energy is and make a new choice.

Become quiet; allow yourself to relax and feel at peace. Ask yourself, "What is my calling?" or "What makes me happy?" Listen. Allow your intuition – the soft whispers in your mind, the deep inner knowing in your heart, the wisdom within – to guide you. Allow the answers to surface. You may have a flash of insight. A resolution to a course of action may unfold as you pay attention to your

"THE HEART HAS ITS REASONS WHICH REASON KNOWS NOT OF."

PASCAL

"GOD IS IN THY HEART, YET THOU SEARCHES FOR HIM IN THE WILDERNESS."

ARJUN

feelings. You might simply realize that you have an answer to your problem: the solution may spring fully formed into your mind.

LISTEN TO YOUR HEART

As you start to encourage your intuitive insights by asking questions and acting on the wisdom you receive, you will be blessed with an abundance of wise intelligence coming to you throughout your day. It is always there to guide you. Begin with your heart. Look deeply into it, and trust what you sense and perceive.

Sometimes your intellect does not know how to handle a difficult situation or to make a life-altering decision, but your heart does. One of the main ways you access your intuitive wisdom is through your heart. The next time you are confused or troubled, ask yourself "What does my heart say?" and listen for the answer. The author Stephen Levine stated it this way, "It may be said that God cannot be known in the mind but only experienced in the heart."

KEEP YOUR HEART OPEN

What does success mean to you? How will you know when you have achieved it? Philosopher and writer Joseph Campbell defines success as the ability to "follow your bliss." It is doing what brings you joy as well as contributing to the happiness and well-being of your friends, family, and community. When you follow the path with a heart, you are following your bliss as well as your divine guidance. You are doing what you came here to do. You will

make a difference in the world. You are utilizing the gift of God's love that resides in your heart through doing what you most enjoy.

You are unique. Listen to your heart and do what it tells you by doing what you love. No one else can live your life and do what you have come here to create and learn. A world is waiting for you

WHAT DOES YOUR HEART SAY?

Here are some questions to ask yourself to assure you are on the path with a heart:

✦

1) Do you feel excited and passionate about a choice you are making? This is one of the primary ways your intuition guides you.

✦

2) Does your decision serve or help others as well as yourself? Any choice that is a true "path of the heart" not only fulfills your goals and desires in some way, it also serves others.

✦

3) When you begin to take action on your choice, do opportunities begin to open up and synchronicities occur? Pay attention to any signs and symbols that show up to indicate that you have taken the right action.

✦

4) Does the decision you make provide you with an occasion to use your unique gifts, abilities, and skills? The path with a heart always uses your particular talents. These are part of your tools to create your destiny in this life.

to start your coaching business, to display your beautiful floral designs, to publish your inspired writing, or to offer encouragement through your wisdom. Whatever you love to do is where you need to focus your choices. The path of the heart is God's way of showing you the direction to follow. It is the path to take to achieve your destiny.

Swami Chidvilasananda, who is a guru in the Siddha Yoga tradition of Hinduism, instructs his followers to ask the question, "What can I give?" He believes that most of us approach life with our hands open saying, "Give me what I want." His idea is that when you keep your heart open and allow yourself to be of service to others you receive true abundance and well being.

Do Not Postpone Your Happiness

Look around you and see all the rich opportunities to truly serve others by asking, "What can I do that needs to be done?" Many acts of the heart take little time or money and can have a huge impact on the receiver. Send a "glad you're in my life" note to a friend, bring a meal to someone who is housebound, tell someone close to you what you appreciate about them, send an anonymous donation to someone you know who is struggling financially, give a gift certificate to a salon for someone who has been under stress and needs a little pampering. The list is endless. You will find as you do these things, your heart opens and more joy, love, and abundance flows in.

You may have read this chapter thinking that if you do all these things, your future will be better than the present. The truth is, your point of

"OUR RELIGION IS THE TRADITION OF OUR ANCESTORS – THE DREAMS OF OUR OLD MEN, GIVEN TO THEM IN THE SOLEMN HOURS OF THE NIGHT BY THE GREAT SPIRIT – AND IT IS WRITTEN IN THE HEARTS OF OUR PEOPLE."

CHIEF SEATTLE

power is in the here and now. Do not postpone your happiness until you find the perfect relationship or your ideal job. Experience the aliveness of each moment; focus on what truly makes you happy, creates love, and brings you gladness – here and now. This is the path of the heart, and I assure you that when you make this path a constant choice you will experience a successful, abundant, and joyful life.

"AND LET THE PEACE OF GOD RULE IN YOUR HEARTS. . . ."

COLOSSIANS 3:15

"ONE WAY WE CAN KNOW THAT WE ARE ALIGNED WITH THE LIFE FORCE THAT IS GOD IS THAT WE FEEL MORE AND MORE ALIVE. NOTICE WHAT GIVES YOU ALIVENESS AND WHAT DIMINISHES YOU, DEADENS AND NUMBS YOU SO THAT YOU ONLY SKIM THE SURFACE OF LIFE. BEGIN TO SAY YES TO WHAT QUICKENS AND ENERGIZES, TO THAT WHICH BRINGS JOY AND GRATITUDE."

MARY MANIN MORRISSEY

LETTING GO OF WHAT HOLDS YOU BACK

Who among us has not experienced being overwhelmed and exhausted when we feel that we just cannot "handle it" a moment more. What do you do when you feel stressed? Most of us assume that stress comes from something external. We say, "If only I had a different boss, my job would be okay." "If only my spouse would help with the chores, I'd be happier." "If only my family was more supportive of me I wouldn't be feeling this anguish."

WHEN YOU ARE STRESSED AND OVER-COMMITTED, YOU KNOW IT. You work seventy hour weeks at the office, yet you cannot catch up. Your friends call and want to get together and you cannot find the time to return their calls, much less have dinner with them. You cannot seem to find time to get to the grocery store in order to make some healthy meals. You go to bed exhausted but you cannot fall asleep. You try to survive on four or five hours of sleep, and you wake up feeling angry, edgy, and irritable. You snap at your kids, your spouse, your staff, other drivers on the way to work – you even snap at your dog. Do you experience any or all of this? Not a pretty picture, is it?

WHAT DRAINS YOU?

Consider your extreme stress in another way, as a signal from your inner guidance that something is out of kilter in your life. Your intuition is telling you to slow down, take a look at the things in your life that exhaust you, and begin to let go of what is doing this to you. In other words, your fatigue, weakness, and depletion add up to a big message from your intuition: take time to reprioritize your life. The negative symptoms are your intuition's attempt to communicate that it is time to focus on what gives you energy and joy and to begin to let go of what drains you.

"WHAT'S TERRIBLE IS TO **PRETEND** THAT THE SECOND-RATE IS **FIRST-RATE.** TO PRETEND THAT YOU **DON'T** NEED LOVE WHEN YOU **DO**; OR YOU LIKE YOUR **WORK** WHEN YOU KNOW QUITE WELL YOU'RE **CAPABLE** OF BETTER."

DORIS LESSING

> "START LIVING NOW. STOP SAVING THE GOOD CHINA FOR THAT SPECIAL OCCASION. STOP WITHHOLDING YOUR LOVE UNTIL THAT SPECIAL PERSON MATERIALIZES. EVERY DAY YOU ARE ALIVE IS A SPECIAL OCCASION. EVERY MINUTE, EVERY BREATH, IS A GIFT FROM GOD."

MARY MANIN MORRISSEY

You can choose to ignore these messages. Many people do. Making any change is hard when you are feeling totally overwhelmed. However, I have observed that when you disregard the clues that tell you your life is out of balance, God simply provides more evidence until a crisis erupts and you are forced to make a change.

FUEL YOUR SPIRIT

Many of us think that God's will is for us to work hard and do "what's right." The message most of us received as we grew up was "You should do this" or "You should not do that" if you want to make it in this world. You certainly were not told to listen carefully to your heart or your inner wisdom and do what it tells you to do!

You have recognized that your life is out of control, and you feel drained and exhausted. So now the important question becomes, "How do I begin to create a life of balance? How do I start the process of beginning to appreciate and enjoy my life again?" Getting clear about your priorities and about what energizes you is the first step. This exercise has a series of questions to help get you started.

Many people deal with stress by simply taking a vacation. Of course, I am a big fan of vacations. But, unless you begin to make some day-to-day changes in your life, you are apt to come back from your time away and feel just as out-of-balance as before you left. Be sure to give yourself some down time every day. I am not talking about huge changes, just some time in your day that gives you some breathing space. It can be little things like taking a walk during your lunch break or leaving the office early in order to shop for and cook a healthy meal. It could be making time for lunch with a friend, or creating time on the weekends where you have nothing planned, scheduling a massage, or listening to relaxing music when you get home.

> "MAINTAINING A COMPLICATED LIFE IS A GREAT WAY TO AVOID CHANGING IT."

ELAINE ST. JAMES

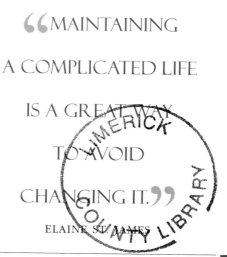

LIMERICK COUNTY LIBRARY

GAINING A BALANCED LIFE

Who or what gives you energy? This is a clue from your inner guidance about what to move towards. These might be people you enjoy being with or things that you enjoy doing. It can be as simple as having time to read a novel or taking a luxurious bath before bedtime. Perhaps you feel energized when you spend time with kids, listen to music, garden, or volunteer for a local service group. Begin to pay attention to the times in your life when you feel enthusiastic, passionate, and full of energy. List a few examples here:

_____

_____

✦

Who or what depletes you? This could be a situation, a habitual pattern of thought, or a person. Anything that enervates you is part of the feedback system from your intuition about what to avoid or to move away from. This might be a negative friend or co-worker, a job that does not serve you, or a way of thinking about your life. If you feel dread, depressed, hopeless, or fearful about someone or something in your life, you are getting a valuable clue that positive change is needed in this area.

_____

_____

✦

What do you NEED to do? Let's face it, if you could be doing anything you wanted you might be lying on a warm beach, eating tropical fruit, and enjoying the sounds of the waves. However, being a practical sort, let's take a look at what you absolutely need to being doing. Everything you listed in the "what drains you" part of this exercise is unlikely to change overnight. You may need to keep your job for now. You may be obligated to care for your ill parents. It is helpful to take a look at those areas in your life that you feel are "must do's" for now. List them here:

_____

_____

✦

What do you love to do? Sometimes we get so caught up in our lives that we forget to ask ourselves this question. For the purpose of this exercise, try to suspend the thought about how you could possibly achieve these dreams. What do you love to do? What you feel empowered, inspired, and excited about is valuable information provided by your inner wisdom. It indicates the direction you need to head. Jot down a few of your thoughts and ideas here:

_____

_____

✦

What's your plan of action? Take a look at the lists that you just created. Some themes probably pop out at you. You will fine some clear indication of something you need to let go of, the areas in your life that obviously depleted you. Also find areas that energize and enliven you. Write about some small (or large, if appropriate) steps that you are willing to take.

_____

_____

"SYNCHRONISTIC EVENTS OCCUR WHEN YOU ARE COMMITTED TO TAKING EXTREMELY GOOD CARE OF YOURSELF.... A DIVINE FORCE RALLIES BEHIND YOU TO SUPPORT YOUR DECISIONS."

CHERYL RICHARDSON

Getting an out-of-control life back into balance is not an overnight task. Writing a list like you have just done and becoming more aware of what depletes you and what gives you energy is a first step. You have some choices you need to make in order to bring about balance.

YOUR INNER MESSAGES

Remember, if you ignore all the messages you receive about your unbalanced life, the universe tends to come in with a bigger communication, saying, in effect, "WARNING! Change needed here! Pay attention!" If the inner messages are disregarded long enough, your body begins to transmit serious signs of discomfort. The headaches, muscle strain, tiredness, knots in your stomach, and ulcers are all familiar ways people experience physical signs of stress.

When you continually harbor negative emotions toward yourself or others, you begin to create a toxic situation in your body as well as in your life as a whole. When your thoughts are full of fear and hate and your life is in full panic mode, you are heading towards a crisis that often results in an illness. When you learn to honor the wisdom of your intuition on a day-to-day basis and act on the information, you will find that your life stays in balance despite the outer circumstances. The writer Somerset Maugham summed it up best when he said, "It's a funny thing about life. If you refuse to accept anything but the best, you very often get it."

"IF YOU GATHERED UP ALL THE FEARFUL THOUGHTS THAT EXIST IN THE MIND OF THE AVERAGE PERSON, LOOKED AT THEM OBJECTIVELY, AND TRIED TO DECIDE JUST HOW MUCH GOOD THEY PROVIDED THAT PERSON, YOU WOULD SEE THAT NOT SOME BUT ALL FEARFUL THOUGHTS ARE USELESS. THEY DO NO GOOD. ZERO. THEY INTERFERE WITH DREAMS, HOPES, DESIRES, AND PROGRESS."

RICHARD CARLSON

FEAR:
THE EDGE
OF YOUR
REALITY

Fear is the biggest hurdle that stops most people from achieving their dreams. Do you know that everyone experiences it? It is what happens when you move out of the comfort zone of the life you have known and into the life on the border of your hopes, dreams, and ambitions. Danaan Perry has written a beautiful essay in which he likens life to a series of trapeze bars: "most of the time, I spend my life hanging on for dear life to my trapeze-bar-of-the-moment." When he is holding onto his current bar he feels in control.

YET, INEVITABLY, LIFE INTERVENES AND REQUIRES THAT HE MOVE TO HIS NEXT TRAPEZE BAR. "It is my next step, my growth, my aliveness coming to get me. In my heart-of-hearts I know that for me to grow, I must release my grip on this present, well-known bar to move to the new one."

COPING WITH FEAR

Fear is the biggest hurdle that stops most of us from achieving our dreams. Many of us feel the fear and say, "I'm not going one step further," "Give me a guarantee of success and then I'll move forward," or even, "I feel scared. This must be my intuition telling me that this direction is wrong."

Many of us choose to stay stuck or simply treading water. We feel safe where we are. We convince ourselves that what we have is not so bad and we talk ourselves out of our dreams.

Do you approach your life with one foot on the brake (your fear) and one foot on the accelerator (your dream)? With that combination you tend to neutralize any forward movement. If you want to move forward in your life, you must release your

"ONE DOESN'T HAVE TO BE HOLY AND HEALED TO EXPERIENCE DIVINE GUIDANCE. IN FACT, SUCH GUIDANCE OFTEN COMES AS A RESULT OF PAIN AND PROBLEMS… WHEN THINGS ARE COASTING ALONG SMOOTHLY, WE DON'T NEED GUIDANCE. THE SUDDEN FLASHES OF INTUITION AND DREAMS WE HAVE IN OUR DARKEST HOURS, HOWEVER, ARE CAPABLE OF RENEWING OUR LIVES, CHANGING OUR COURSE, AND MENDING A BROKEN SPIRIT."

JOAN BORYSENKO

brake. Courage is what it takes to face your fears. When you use your connection with your inner guidance it gives you courage.

As you take action on your dreams you may feel as if you are on the edge of a cliff. You are about to take a leap of faith, and no one is there to catch you. But you are not alone. The inspiration and direction from your intuition is there to guide you safely to your hopes and dreams. The voice of God exists in each of us. We often do not ask for help. We have not built a relationship with our inner guidance, while it is too bad because it can be like a best friend whispering encouragement and direction whenever we need it.

FEAR VERSUS INTUITION

When you take a step in a new direction you are bound to feel uncomfortable. It is scary. You are likely to feel anxious. You are in a situation where you have never been before. Newness is a mixed bag. It can make you feel wildly excited and open to experiences and ideas you might never have considered. But it can also make you fearful. Everything suddenly feels unfamiliar. You are in strange territory without a map to get you to your next destination. Sometimes you may not even know what that next destination is. It may help to know that almost everyone feels afraid and anxious when trying new things. It is okay to be afraid; it is natural. The most important thing is to not let your fear be a big "stop sign" in your life.

One of the questions I am asked most frequently when lecturing is: "How do I tell the difference between my fear and my intuition?" I think that whole issue of whether it is fear, anxiety, paranoia, or intuition is often complicated! I have found it takes practice and the ability to be in touch with your feelings.

For example, when I was asked to write *The Complete Idiot's Guide to Being Psychic* in the summer of 1998, I felt happy and excited about it. These feelings indicated to me that my inner guidance was saying, "This is a good thing. Go do it." I also felt anxious and scared. Could I write well? Could I work with a deadline?

> **❝WE CANNOT ESCAPE FEAR. WE CAN ONLY TRANSFORM IT INTO A COMPANION THAT ACCOMPANIES US ON ALL OUR EXCITING ADVENTURES. TAKE A RISK A DAY – ONE SMALL OR BOLD STROKE THAT WILL MAKE YOU FEEL GREAT ONCE YOU HAVE DONE IT.❞**
>
> SUSAN JEFFERS

So I had to decide which of those feelings to trust. I knew from past experience that I often felt a little anxious when I started a new project: this was a familiar feeling. It felt very different from the depressed, "I don't want to do this" feeling I get when my intuition is saying, "This is not the right path for you!"

HOW DO YOU KNOW?

The tough thing about intuition is that you know but you do not know how you know, and sometimes you do not even know what you know! Let me explain. I suggest breaking your decision down into smaller steps, if possible. That way it will not feel so overwhelming, and you probably will not feel so anxious. I have found that when you take small steps towards what your intuition is indicating, doors often open. This is the God's way of saying, "You made a good decision." Your other option is to stand still and never move at all. I do not recommend that alternative!

Sometimes, making a bold move – a BIG step, a leap of faith – is important. Only then can you understand through experience that God can be

MOVING BEYOND YOUR FEAR

List four successes that you are proud of achieving:

....

....

....

....

✦

Describe what led up to each of those situations. Things to consider: Were you scared or anxious at any point on the path to your success? How did you overcome that fear? What role did your intuition play in helping you achieve your goal?

....

....

....

✦

What qualities do you feel you developed as the result of these successes?

....

....

✦

What other good things came about as the result of these achievements?

....

....

....

....

✦

In looking back, what were the key factors that made you successful?

....

....

....

....

✦

How could you apply what you have learned in this exercise to move towards a new goal in your life?

....

....

....

trusted to provide safety. The Rolling Stones song "You Can't Always Get What You Want" comes to mind here. The chorus is, "You can't always get what you want. But if you try sometimes, you get what you need."

If you are in a anxiety-producing situation that has been going on for awhile, try to look at it in a different way. Most of us succumb to self-pity, "Why did this happen to me?" "What did I do to deserve this?" Unfortunately that kind of thinking drains all of your positive energy and just makes you feel bad and keeps you stuck. Tell yourself, "I want to see this situation in a new way. Maybe I can't see the good at this very moment, but I believe I'll come to understand it."

KNOW AND RELEASE YOUR FEAR

Fear can be useful to you. In the best circumstances fear is there to warn you that you are taking a risk and should be prepared. Many of us, when we receive a "fear message," simply say, "I'm afraid. Guess I shouldn't take this risk." How about turning this around? As you recognize that you are afraid, anxious, and on edge, try speaking to your fear directly: "I know you, Fear. I know that you are here to protect me. I am open to what you have to tell me so I can prepare, but I will not let you guide my life." The point is to acknowledge your fear. Anything that you resist only grows larger. Accept your fear. It is part of your psychology, and

> **"YOU MAY HAVE A FRESH START ANY MOMENT YOU CHOOSE, FOR THIS THING WE CALL FAILURE IS NOT THE FALLING DOWN, BUT THE STAYING DOWN."**
>
> MARY PICKFORD

> **"TO CONQUER FEAR IS THE BEGINNING OF WISDOM."**
>
> BERTRAND RUSSELL

it is there for a reason, but you do not need to be ruled by it.

If fear is your constant companion and stops you from achieving your goals, you may need to shift your focus and ask for your inner guidance to help you with this. Here is a prayer to try. As always, be sure to alter the words to fit what you need.

> *I know that I am filled with fear and anxiety right now. I know that I have dreams that I want to achieve. My fear is standing in my way. I know that I need help moving beyond this fear. I believe in your power to heal. Please help me to allow your guidance so that I can receive strength and energy to reach for my dreams. I allow your guidance to direct my life through my intuition. With this power I can move forward toward my dreams."*

Anyone who has a dream knows fear. Part of the requirement of making your dream come alive is to step beyond the borders of your fear. I have found that any dream worth following produces some fear and anxiety for me. The bigger my fear, the more exciting, and ultimately life enhancing, is my dream.

Gerald Jampolsky, MD, wrote in his book *Teach Only Love*, "There are only two emotions: love, our natural inheritance, and fear, an invention of our minds which is illusory. Each instant of the day we choose between these two, and our choice determines the kind of day we have and how we will perceive the world." Trust that the power that guides the universe guides your life. Ask for God's wisdom to assist you to release your fears in order for you to achieve your dreams.

"VIEW ANY AND ALL OBSTACLES AS LESSONS, NOT INDICATIONS OF FAILURE. KEEP IN MIND THAT YOU ARE PRACTICING PATIENCE AND DETACHMENT FROM OUTCOME. WHEN ANYTHING APPEARS TO BE AN OBSTACLE, DO NOT USE THAT MATERIAL FACT TO DENY THE EXISTENCE OF THE UNIVERSAL ENERGY THAT IS YOUR ESSENCE… EVERYTHING THAT SHOWS UP IN YOUR LIFE IS SUPPOSED TO. THIS INCLUDES THE FALLS IN YOUR LIFE, WHICH PROVIDE YOU WITH THE ENERGY TO PROPEL YOURSELF TO A HIGHER STATE OF AWARENESS."

WAYNE DYER

WHAT HAPPENS WHEN YOU DON'T GET WHAT YOU WANT?

There are moments in everyone's life when they do not know whether to abandon their goals or continue to be patient and endure the uncertainty. This is a very painful place to be. You may be wracked with guilt and indecision. "Should I continue or should I give it up? Maybe I'm doing something wrong." Whatever reasons you may come up with, the cry to God can be summed up as: "I've tried everything I know to make this dream happen and nothing's working!"

EVERYONE FACES A TIME WHEN THE THING THEY MOST WANT seems to be beyond their reach. This might be a relationship, a job, more money, or better health. Being unable to attain a long-sought goal can be lonely and frightening. The fear we experience goes beyond the mere fact that the goal has not been achieved. The fear makes us ask ourselves, "Do we really have any control over our life experience?"

WE ARE HERE TO LEARN

We all have different belief systems about how to attain what we want in life. For some of us that may include affirmations and visualizations. Others may believe that through their hard work and sacrifice they will eventually achieve their just rewards. Many others believe in luck, fate or, "karma". Some think that going to the therapist enough times to work out issues can help. Please understand that I am not criticizing any of these paths; they have their place in working toward a balanced life.

I see many clients who are on a spiritual path. They are seekers trying to find God. I believe there are many ways to find and experience a connection

THE SURRENDER PRAYER

Here's a prayer that I pray when I struggle
with achieving my goals:

✦

Dear God:
If this dream I have is for my highest good, please
show me a way to achieve it. Help me to have
passion for this dream, to have courage and
persistence. If this dream will not benefit me and
others, redirect me. I surrender this concern to
you and ask you to fill me with peace.
Amen

the suffering and heartache that comes from difficult times and circumstances, we often come to know God. On those occasions when we are in the most pain and are at our most vulnerable, we finally surrender. A tremendous peace comes with knowing we do not have to control it all, that we truly are going to be okay, that no matter what the outer circumstances we will be whole again.

FACING DIFFICULTIES

I see clients when they are struggling with indecision or losing sight of their dreams. Many people assume that if they walk on the "right" spiritual path, they will feel wonderful all the time. They will be in perfect health and have a relationship with their heaven-sent soul mate; money will flow from above at all times; and their children will be perfect and well adjusted.

Well, dream on. The reality is that parts of building our dreams are difficult and raise issues about ourselves that we came here to confront. We are all here to learn love, compassion, forgiveness, patience, persistence, courage, faith, and a whole host of other wonderful qualities that most of us have forgotten. Just because our dreams do not show up exactly as we imagined does not mean that they will not come true. The dark night of the soul that you may be experiencing could be part of a passage to an even larger dream.

Chaos and indecision are natural parts of building your dreams. Faith is sometimes built step by step. Your goal is not necessarily to create each dream exactly as you imagined it. Your goal is to have a balanced life of love and compassion for yourself and those around you, despite your

with God. The one common denominator I see is that at some point all of them come to what I call "The Surrender Moment." This is the time when they acknowledge that all of the affirmations, hard work, struggle, therapy have not given them their cherished goal. They come to see me and ask, "Why is this happening to me?" and they wonder if they are being possibly punished by a God that is unhappy with them.

This is often the hardest question for me to answer. What I do know is this: there is a wisdom and love that flows through us and animates our world, and it does have a reason. When I have a client in my office sitting unhappily in front of me who has literally "tried everything" to bring about a goal, I ask them to consider letting go of control over the outcome. In other words, surrender that control.

In our limited human capacity we may not understand what purpose is being served in our struggle. I do know that we are here on this earth to learn about compassion, forgiveness, love, mercy, faith, and tolerance. Through

"GOD'S DELAYS ARE NOT HIS DENIALS."

BETH MENDE CONNY

circumstances. That is a tall order, but God constantly puts lessons in your path until you achieve those qualities.

The answer to the question "What am I here to learn?" is within you. You came into this life knowing your mission and life purpose. Very rarely is the answer something concrete. "You're here to find a cure for AIDS," or "Your mission is to be the President of the United States." Instead, the mission statements that I hear in my readings with clients are along the lines of "Carol has come into this life to hone her healing abilities through understanding and experiencing forgiveness and compassion," or "John has chosen this life to learn lessons about faith, trust, and love." You are presented with lessons that you have come here to learn, unlearn, or relearn.

WHEN YOU FEEL STUCK

You are not a victim of these life situations, even though you may feel that way. Try viewing yourself as a student of the difficulty you are facing. Begin the habit of asking, "What is it that I am here to learn?" So often, people ask the wrong questions, as if they were victims: "Why is this happening to me?" or "What am I doing wrong?" Can you feel the difference in the first question and the last two?

Try utilizing your inner guidance to help you when you feel stuck in a difficult situation. Ask questions like, "What do I need to learn?", "How could I view this situation differently?", and "What is the best possible outcome for this situation?" The answer may not always leap into your mind. Sometimes it takes awhile to retrain your thinking, as well as to listen to those subtle inner messages

> **"THINK OF USING ALL OBSTACLES AS STEPPING STONES TO BUILD THE LIFE YOU WANT."**
>
> MARSHA SINETAR

> **"LIFE IS FUNDAMENTALLY A MATTER OF GROWING, A GROWTH EXPERIENCE. MISSING THE MARK IS ONE OF THE WAYS IN WHICH WE LEARN TO HIT THE TARGET. FAILURE IS A VITAL PART OF ACHIEVING SUCCESS.... SETBACKS, EVEN FAILURES, MAY BE AN IMPORTANT PART OF THAT LEARNING."**
>
> ERIC BUTTERWORTH

from your guidance system. The answer may come as an impulse to try something different or as a gradual awakening to a new way of thinking about an obstacle you are confronting.

SETBACKS ARE NORMAL

Rosalind Russell said, "Flops are part of life's menu and I'm never a girl to miss out on a course!" She understood that we often reach success through a series of ups and downs. When you are in a "down" place and feel stuck, know that it usually does not last long. You are perfectly fine just the way you are. You are simply in a transition.

Obstacles and setbacks are often placed in your path to allow new learning to unfold. They are there to enable you to develop new skills or fresh ways of perceiving life before you take the next step. Learn to be patient with yourself. Find some ways to enjoy your life despite the lull and continue to focus on what you want. There is almost always a space between your dreams and reality. But if you can imagine that reality you can make it so.

"GRATITUDE, LIKE FAITH, IS A MUSCLE. THE MORE YOU USE IT, THE STRONGER IT GROWS, AND THE MORE POWER YOU HAVE TO USE IT ON YOUR BEHALF. IF YOU DO NOT PRACTICE GRATEFULNESS, ITS BENEFACTION WILL GO UNNOTICED, AND YOUR CAPACITY TO DRAW ON ITS GIFTS WILL BE DIMINISHED. TO BE GRATEFUL IS TO FIND BLESSINGS IN EVERYTHING. THIS IS THE MOST POWERFUL ATTITUDE TO ADOPT, FOR THERE ARE BLESSINGS IN EVERYTHING."

ALAN COHEN

THE WISDOM OF GRATITUDE

When I was in my early thirties, I went back to school to study for my Masters Degree in Education. When I thought about going to school, I was quite excited and grateful for the opportunity. However, my first semester was not the thrilling occasion I had hoped. "This isn't fun," I told myself. "This is hard work. I don't know if I can take this for three years."

IN A WORD, I WAS MISERABLE. I WAS OVERWHELMED BY THE FACT THAT I HAD SIGNED ON for what was a three-year program. "Three years out of my life," I kept saying almost like a mantra. I felt lonely and filled with self-pity.

Fortunately, after meditation one day, a new thought occurred to me. "Lynn, this isn't three years out of your life. This is three years of your life, and you have the choice to make this a fun experience or an awful one. The choice is yours." That marked my new adventure in graduate school. I was determined to turn my attitude around and be grateful for the experience. I thought about what I wanted to learn and what was fun for me. I resolved to make some friends instead of seeing everyone as somehow different from me. It became a new experience through my shift in attitude. The insight that dawned on me was that the school did not need to change — my attitude did. It made all the difference in the world.

Melodie Beattie said, "Gratitude unlocks the fullness of life. It turns what we have into enough

> **"IN OUR DAILY LIVES, WE MUST SEE THAT IT IS NOT HAPPINESS THAT MAKES US GRATEFUL, BUT THE GRATEFULNESS THAT MAKES US HAPPY."**
>
> ALBERT CLARKE

and more.... It can turn a meal into a feast, a house into a home, a stranger into a friend. Gratitude makes sense of our past, brings peace for today, and creates a vision for tomorrow."

What are you grateful for? You have a terrific opportunity to live your life with joy no matter what your circumstances. You do not have to postpone happiness until you have the relationship you want, or all your bills are paid, or your dream job falls into your lap. Joy does not exist out in the world somewhere. Joy is an inside job. The way to create more joy in your life is by having an abundance of gratitude.

When I first began giving readings, I struggled a great deal with understanding why bad things happen to good people. I still have not reached a full understanding about this issue, but what I do know is this: you may not be able to change your life circumstance, but you can change your thoughts and attitudes about it. This is the one truth that can make your life heaven or hell. You do not have a choice that your husband or wife died; you do not have a choice that you had a child with a birth defect; you do not have a choice that

you were injured in an accident. What you do have a choice about is how you respond to these circumstances.

POTENTIAL FOR TRANSFORMATION

Any crisis can hold within it the dynamic potential for personal and spiritual transformation if you allow it. Many people get stuck in a frightful nightmare when something terrible happens in their lives. They see no way out of their misery. They are stuck in an endless cycle of desperation and emptinessin which they seemingly have no power and no control. However, at these times when they feel they have nothing left to lose, they begin to find the first intimations of faith, the faint shadings of a thread of hope that may bring them back from the edge of despair.

When stuck in a pattern of anger, victimization, and hopelessness, you feel disconnected from the source of power that can help you. You shut it out and believe that no possibility of healing or salvation can exist. While there is no one "right way" back from this difficult place, each painful transition invites you to allow for the possibility that there is a God, a kind, wise, and loving energy that not only guides you through the transition you seek but also helps create a transformation in your life.

A TOOL FOR CHANGE

People often expect the answer to their prayers to be an immediate and positive change in their circumstances, a miracle perhaps. Sometimes this occurs. More often, it does not. When you ask for guidance from God a profound change begins to occur. You may feel drawn to a book that makes you feel better by altering your point of view. You might feel inspired to talk to a friend who has the sensitive understanding to move you in a new direction. A new opportunity presents itself where none seemed to exist before. Little by little a new path is made clear.

I believe that an attitude of gratitude can turn the most difficult life circumstances into a blessing. I have a colleague, Ann Durrum Robinson, who is an 86-year-old intuition and creativity consultant. She is probably one of the most resilient people I know.

"IF YOU CONCENTRATE ON FINDING WHATEVER IS GOOD IN EVERY SITUATION, YOU WILL DISCOVER THAT YOUR LIFE WILL SUDDENLY BE FILLED WITH GRATITUDE, A FEELING THAT NURTURES THE SOUL."

RABBI HAROLD KUSHNER

She calls herself the "Chairwoman of the Bored." She gives wonderful talks from her "winged wheelchair." (I call her the best "sit down" comic around.) She earns her living from talks such as, "Bad Times Made Verse" or "What to Do When Life Goes to the Doggerel, a Study in Re-silly-ence."

Have you ever noticed how difficult it is to allow wise, loving, inner guidance to flow through you when you are angry and upset? Gratitude is a powerful tool for beginning to change your negative emotions to more positive ones. You begin right where you are, no matter what your circumstances. Expressing appreciation starts the dynamic shift from resistant energy to a more open and flowing place where new possibilities and options exist.

"GRATITUDE IS A FORM OF WISDOM. IT IS PATIENT, LOVING, HOPEFUL, AND RIGOROUSLY HONEST. IT DENIES NOTHING, AND IT OVERLOOKS NOTHING. IT LOOKS REALITY FULL IN THE FACE AND SAYS, "THIS IS TRUE, THIS IS ME, THIS IS MY SITUATION, AND I HAVE THE OPPORTUNITY TO BUILD FROM HERE. THIS IS MY STARTING POINT, AND I WILL SUCCEED!"

PHIL HUMBERT

OPENING YOUR HEART TO GRATITUDE

There are numerous ways to foster an abundance of gratitude. The stream of openness and love begins when you open your heart to give without expecting anything in return.

◆

Begin to let others know that you care about them.

◆

Practice random acts of kindness.

◆

Send flowers when it is not a birthday or other special occasion.

◆

Write a gratitude note to a friend, listing all the things you like and admire about them.

◆

Listen to someone without judgement.

◆

Visit someone who is housebound.

◆

Send an anonymous donation of money to a person in need.

◆

Start a gratitude journal.

WHAT ARE YOU GRATEFUL FOR?

Faith is a big component of the next step. You trust that God has a message for you, that a solution is at hand even though you cannot see it right now. Gratitude sets into motion the right consciousness for opening up to the flow of grace and goodness.

While I am lying in bed at night I drift off to sleep by reviewing my day. I think about what I experienced as the highlights. Yesterday, the two kids who live across the street from me, three-year-old Kristina and seven year-old Devan, rang my doorbell and came in to visit. We sat in my kitchen talking, eating cookies, and drinking milk. Kristina chatted excitedly about a new dress her mother had purchased for her and Devan spoke about a science project he was involved in at school. When I thought about my day, that was the part I was most grateful for. The whole visit lasted perhaps five minutes before they were on to their next activity.

Sophy Burnham wrote, "We all have angels guiding us.... They look after us. They heal us, touch us, comfort us with invisible warm hands . . . What will bring their help? Asking. Giving thanks." Focusing on what I am grateful for helps me become more aware in the moment that it is happening. I may even have the thought, "I wonder if this moment will be the thing that I most appreciate today? I should savor this."

THE GIFT OF LIFE

Sometimes the answer surprises me. It is usually something very simple. I enjoyed watching a sunset, or I had a great conversation with a friend, or the walk that I took earlier in the evening with my husband made me appreciate him. I feel more present and alive. This moment is a gift of life. It is a moment when I am aware of God and I am grateful to be alive.

> **"EVERYTHING HAS ITS WONDERS, EVEN DARKNESS AND SILENCE, AND I LEARN, WHATEVER STATE I MAY BE IN, THEREIN TO BE CONTENT."**
>
> HELEN KELLER

"EVERYTHING WE DO IS INFUSED WITH THE ENERGY WITH WHICH WE DO IT. IF WE'RE FRANTIC, LIFE WILL BE FRANTIC. IF WE'RE PEACEFUL, LIFE WILL BE PEACEFUL. AND SO OUR GOAL IN ANY SITUATION BECOMES INNER PEACE. OUR INTERNAL STATE DETERMINES OUR EXPERIENCE OF OUR LIVES; OUR EXPERIENCES DO NOT DETERMINE OUR INTERNAL STATE."

MARIANNE WILLIAMSON

REPLENISH YOUR SOUL

What comes to your mind when you think of "taking care of yourself?" Pause a moment and really think about it... Is it a long vacation by the beach? Endless massages? A full month at a restorative spa? Perhaps you imagine that you can do that when you retire. Most of us think of taking time out of our lives in order to really nurture ourselves. But what would your life look and feel like if you had balance, peace, and calm as an everyday experience? What if you did not need to get away from your daily life in order to take care of your soul? In our contemporary life we have so few occasions for reflection. Yet this is where restorative, spiritual change and inner guidance frequently take place. This sort of time used to be very common. It just naturally happened in the spaces between the events of our lives.

SITTING ON THE PORCH AFTER DINNER, RIDING A BIKE TO WORK OR SCHOOL, OR TAKING A LEISURELY WALK during our lunch break all provide nourishment for the body as well as for the soul. Tranquil moments come when waiting for the pot to boil, the rain to stop, the casserole to bake in the oven. Those no longer happen as frequently or as easily, and people long for them. That is the natural rhythm of life.

NURTURE YOURSELF

Several years ago I met a client named Helen. She was an in her mid-thirties, quite well-dressed, and attractive – and terribly overwhelmed. I remember trying to give her a reading. Every time I suggested a new or different way of approaching an issue or situation in her life, Helen would let me know it simply was not possible because she had so much to do!

She had quite a litany of reasons why she could not possibly slow down or create any change in her life. She had kids to take care of, her mother-in-law who was ill, and her unfulfilling full-time job with overtime. I felt drained as I listened to her describe it all. I became aware that everything Helen recited was about taking care of the needs of others. This highly intelligent woman who was heading for a nervous breakdown.

All of Helen's energy, thinking, and beliefs were focused on accomplishing more, having more, and doing it all perfectly. When I asked her how she nurtured herself, she took a long pause. She looked at me blankly, then finally said, "I never stopped to think about that."

> ❝FOR I DO NOTHING BUT GO ABOUT PERSUADING YOU ALL, OLD AND YOUNG ALIKE, NOT TO TAKE THOUGHT FOR YOUR PERSONS OR YOUR PROPERTIES, BUT FIRST AND CHIEFLY TO CARE ABOUT THE GREATEST IMPROVEMENTS OF THE SOUL.❞

PLATO

The assignment I gave to Helen was for her to begin to think about what it was that gave her energy and what it was that drained her. What did she long for? What could she let go of in order to create more balance? What did she feel passionate and enthusiastic about? She later reported that our conversation was one of the most meaningful she had ever had. No one had ever asked her what was important to her, and she had never asked herself.

Have you found yourself getting so caught up in the frustrations of your job, driving your kids to their various after school programs, making meals, and struggling with life that you forget to ask yourself, "What's my true purpose here?" Perhaps like Helen, you are afraid to ask yourself that question. Dr. Richard D. Dobbins states it this way, "Until the pain of remaining the same hurts more than the pain of change, most people prefer to remain the same."

When will you begin tuning into your own soul and listening to its wisdom? Do you get so caught up in the "busy-ness" of your life that you neglect to give yourself permission for emotional, physical, and spiritual renewal? But it is during those times that you remember what is meaningful. John

Wanamaker writes, "People who cannot find time for recreation are obliged sooner or later to find time for illness." Taking the time to nurture yourself when you are well and healthy is much more pleasant. Are you willing to begin?

RESTORE PEACE

Begin to create a pace that feels good to you, that feels like life is flowing for you, not hectic and out of control. If you are peaceful and choose to live your life with balance, your life will be peaceful. When you constantly feel tired, cranky, and out of sorts, your inner guidance is working over-time to catch your attention. It is saying, "Warning! Your life is seriously out-of-balance!" God is providing the course correction for you by cautioning that the path you are on is leading to energy depletion.

You cannot do it all. Let that be okay. You are only human like all the rest of us! Your task is to recognize when your life is out of balance and, as quickly as possible, do what you can to nurture yourself and restore flow and ease. How long do you want to wait to start living "the good life?" Your intuition constantly points to the path that will lead you there.

When you take care of yourself and take time to do what you love, you are in balance. You have time and space to once again feel and appreciate the fullness and richness of your life. Allow yourself time for prayer and meditation – the one thing you can do that allows you to experience the presence of God. You can gain access to all the possible resources of healing guidance for your mind, body, and spirit.

> ❝EVERYONE SHOULD KNOW THAT YOU CAN'T LIVE IN ANY OTHER WAY THAN BY CULTIVATING THE SOUL.❞

THOMAS MOORE

REGENERATING YOUR BODY, MIND, AND SPIRIT

If you have read this far you know that following your passion and enthusiasm is a way of honoring your inner guidance. What do you love to do that is fun and creative? What is the best way for you to take time for contemplation? How can you make more time for those activities that are truly regenerative instead of enervating. These occasions allow pleasant, slow-down time to soothe your spirits. They are gifts from God to help replenish ourself. If I have not listed your favorites here, please write them in the extra spaces. Your goal is three-fold: 1) To become aware of what nurtures you. 2) To be honest with yourself about the last time you took the time to do this activity. 3) To create an action plan for making the time to do these things in your life.

✦

ARTISTIC AND CREATIVE ENDEAVORS
(Writing, painting, cooking, drawing, dancing, singing, hobbies, crafts)

Favorite activity	When did you last do it?	Action plan for doing this activity more:

PERSONAL TIME
(Prayer, journal writing, spend time in nature, meditation, resting, daydreaming, inspirational reading, gardening, time away (spa, retreat), spiritual class or service)

Favorite activity	When did you last do it?	Action plan for doing this activity more:

SOCIAL TIME
(Talking with friends, volunteering, hosting a dinner party, going to a music event, seeing a play, meal with a friend)

Favorite activity	When did you do it last?	Action plan for doing this activity more:

PHYSICAL ACTIVITIES
(Yoga, tai chi, racket sports, swimming, skating, running, skiing, team sports)

Favorite activity	When did you do it last?	Action plan for doing this activity more:

"SET YOUR INTENTION, AND TRUST THE UNIVERSE TO TAKE CARE OF THE DETAILS."

MIKE FOTHERINGHAM

A WEALTH OF HELP TO CREATE A LIFE YOU LOVE

I am a pretty busy person. I thrive on doing a lot of projects all at the same time. While I am writing this book, I am also consulting with clients, conducting workshops, sending out tape orders, writing newsletters and articles, spending time with my family, promoting my other books, etc. You may not have the same things on your "To Do" list as I do on mine, but I hope you will find my approach helpful.

A COUPLE OF YEARS AGO I HAD A PERIOD OF A FEW MONTHS WHEN I FELT TOTALLY OVERWHELMED. I was trying to do everything. My life felt quite out of balance and I began to see this as a sign from my intuition that I needed to pay attention. A new path was emerging, and I felt that I wanted to make space for it to come forth. The strongest impression I had when I meditated was the desire to cut back on my client sessions and to write a book. Typically, you start a book by writing a proposal, then sending it to agents. If an agent likes the book proposal then a long process of pitching the book idea to potential publishers begins. Usually you meet with a lot of rejection.

I already felt that I was doing too much, and the process of shepherding a book through a long, arduous process just seemed to tip me over the edge! I kept asking my intuition what I could do to get my life back in balance. I meditated on this for several days and heard a little voice say, "Let us help."

What often happens to me when I get intuitive impressions is that a whole cluster of information pops into my head at once. What I understood

"WE CAN COUNT ON THAT PRESENCE WHICH MAKES ITSELF KNOWN THROUGH FEELINGS, DREAMS, AND SYNCHRONICITIES. INTUITION IS A NATURAL STATE OF CONSCIOUSNESS IN WHICH OUR SMALL ISOLATED MIND OPENS TO THE BIG MIND OF THE DIVINE."

JOAN BORYSENKO

with those three words was that there was a wealth of help or helpers in the form of guides or angels out there waiting to be of assistance. The image that came to mind was a staff of willing employees waiting in the wings. I laughed out loud when I realized I had a group of guides as my built-in staff, and they were telling me they were underemployed!

HOLD A VISION OF SUCCESS

To more fully understand this concept, contemplate all the events that happen each and every day that you do not even have to think about. They simply happen by themselves. Suppose you were assigned the job of Master of the Universe. What do you think your "To Do" list would look like each day?

✦ Make sure the sun comes up at the beginning of each day.
✦ See to it that the grass is growing.
✦ Don't let it snow in the Southern Hemisphere in the middle of July.
✦ Make sure the sun sets at the appropriate time for each time zone.
✦ Check to see that gravity still works.

You get the idea. One Zen master says, "Spring comes and the grass grows all by itself." There are zillions of things that miraculously work each day without your having to do a single thing to make them happen. Wouldn't you like to put this power to work for you in helping you reach your goals?

I believe that God provides us with endlessly bountiful and infinitely creative resources to help us achieve what we are here to learn and accomplish. The reasons we do not use this gift of providence are multifold. One is that we usually think we have to do it all by ourselves. We get so overwhelmed we usually stop before we start. Also, most of us find it easier to complain about what we do not have than to do something about it. When we do that we block out the guidance that could so easily shift our perspective to a new and more helpful direction.

Have you ever spent time with a successful person? They do not usually expend too much

> ❝AS WE SEEK TO LIVE THE LIFE AND FOLLOW THE WAYS OF BEING THAT ARE MOST ALIGNED WITH GOD AND OUR HIGHER DESTINY, OUR ANGELS ARE DRAWN MORE CLOSELY TO GUIDE AND COUNSEL US.❞
>
> ALMA DANIEL, ET AL

energy on questions like, "Why can't I get what I want?" or "What is it about my childhood that causes me to be a failure?" Instead, they put forth a clear request: "I want to achieve THIS:..." (Fill in the blank.) They hold in their mind's eye a vision of the achievement of their goal. Most successful people do not get too caught up in the small details. They look at the big picture and know that a path will be created to get to where they want to go.

ASSISTANCE FROM THE UNIVERSE

I believe that at the very moment when a clear desire is formed, your guides and angels start gathering their forces to begin the process of moving energy to create the materialization and realization of that goal.

As I mentioned at the beginning of this chapter, several years ago I wanted to write a book but was overwhelmed with the notion of the process. I had a strong resistance to doing any of the "normal" things a person typically does in order to get a book published. I felt guided to simply honor my feelings and just begin writing.

To the right is a sample of a "To Do" list from a period before the publication of my book *The Complete Idiot's Guide to Being Psychic*. After about three months of writing, I received a call from a woman saying she was representing *The Complete Idiot's Guides*. She asked that I return her call and left her number. I must confess that I had heard about the *Dummies* series but not the *Complete Idiot's Guides* at that time. I thought it was someone playing a joke on me. When she called a third time she actually reached me. Imagine my surprise when I learned that she wanted to speak to me about publishing the very book I had begun to write! My guides and angels had been hard at work!

In his book *Real Magic*, Wayne Dyer addresses the existence of this invisible world. He writes, "In every age and civilization, three ideas about life and beyond seem to overlap. The first is that there's an infinite, invisible world beyond the world that we experience. The second is that this infinite world is a part of every human personality. And the third is that the purpose of life is to discover this infinite world."

So, how about you? What do you need help with in your life? Is there something that you have been struggling to create but the path seems filled with obstacles? On the following page is an exercise to do so that you can get some assistance from the Universe in order to achieve your mission.

MY SAMPLE "TO DO" LIST

MY "TO DO"	GUIDES AND ANGELS TO DO
Write a chapter about inner guides	Find an ideal publisher for my book
Send out tape orders	Find a terrific administrative assistant
Begin to create a press kit	Find a positive, successful PR person
Send class info to The Learning Society	Help with the success of the book

"EACH HAS GUARDIAN ANGELS BEFORE HIM AND BEHIND HIM, WHO WATCH HIM BY GOD'S COMMAND."

THE KORAN

> *"WITH INTUITION, WE KNOW WHAT WE NEED TO KNOW, RIGHT WHEN WE NEED TO KNOW IT. THE UNIVERSE, IT SEEMS, DOESN'T WASTE TIME OR ENERGY. INTUITION PRESENTS INFORMATION TO US WHEN WE NEED IT, NOT A MOMENT TOO SOON OR TOO LATE, AND USES ANY MEANS AVAILABLE TO REACH US."*

PENNEY PEIRCE

ASK FOR GUIDANCE

Here is how I work with my requests for helpers in my prayers and meditations: "God, I would like help in having my book published. I feel excited about writing this book and I trust that you are speaking to me through my enthusiasm for this project. If this is the path I should follow please send me signs and acknowledgement. Show me the right path. Allow me to receive assistance from your guides and helpers. Give me the wisdom to notice when this support arrives. Give me patience, strength, love, and courage as I follow this new path to my purpose. Amen."

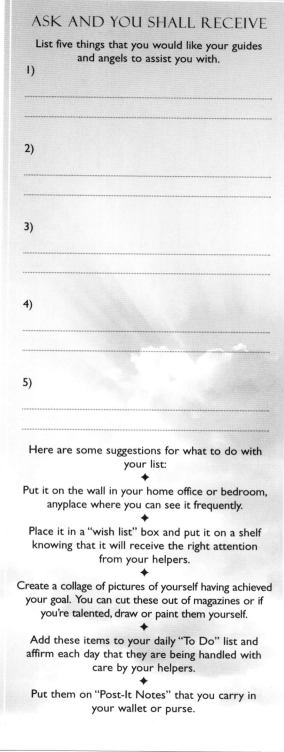

ASK AND YOU SHALL RECEIVE

List five things that you would like your guides and angels to assist you with.

1)

2)

3)

4)

5)

Here are some suggestions for what to do with your list:

✦

Put it on the wall in your home office or bedroom, anyplace where you can see it frequently.

✦

Place it in a "wish list" box and put it on a shelf knowing that it will receive the right attention from your helpers.

✦

Create a collage of pictures of yourself having achieved your goal. You can cut these out of magazines or if you're talented, draw or paint them yourself.

✦

Add these items to your daily "To Do" list and affirm each day that they are being handled with care by your helpers.

✦

Put them on "Post-It Notes" that you carry in your wallet or purse.

"BE AFRAID
OF NOTHING.
YOU HAVE
WITHIN YOU
ALL WISDOM,
ALL POWER,
ALL STRENGTH,
ALL UNDER-
STANDING."

EILEEN CADDY

YOUR INNER GUIDE KNOWS

We live in challenging times. How can you find the wise answers to the decisions you face when the issues are often complex and overwhelming? You may be trying to figure out how to deal with an ill mother while working full-time and trying to be a good parent to your own children. Perhaps you are pondering a career change at mid-life and wish someone could guarantee it will all work out.

YOU MAY BE OVERWHELMED WITH DEBT AND FEEL PARALYZED WITH FEAR ABOUT THE FUTURE. Whatever difficulty you are facing, know that you have a powerful inner guidance system to assist you.

As you listen for guidance on a daily basis you will find yourself presented with one step at a time. Your intuition never gives you more than you can handle. The answer may come through an inspired idea, an image that forms in your mind, or a sudden insight that offers a new and creative direction for you to pursue. When you consistently look within asking, "What is the right course of action?" or "What path should I take?" you will be rewarded with wise, divine guidance.

Your friends and family may help you as they listen and give feedback about your choices and options. You may find books to read on the subject of your dilemma. But only you know the answer that is right for you. Other people can assist you, but when your heart resonates with a, "Yes, this is right!" answer, only you know it.

The right answer for you will be one that makes you feel joyful or excited. Many people feel

"INTUITION IS NOT A STARTLING GIFT THAT IS THE PROVINCE OF A FEW PSYCHICS. IT IS LESS ABOUT DIVINING THE FUTURE THAN IT IS ABOUT ENTERING MORE AUTHENTICALLY INTO THE PRESENT. INTUITION IS ALWAYS OPERATIVE, SO COMMON THAT IT OFTEN EVADES CONSCIOUS RECOGNITION."

JOAN BORYSENKO

confused and wonder how to differentiate the voice of the ego or personality from their intuitive voice or guidance. Other times people worry with the question, "How can I know it is my guidance and not just wishful thinking – or worse yet, fear?"

Messages from your ego or intellect tend to be based on thoughts of scarcity, guilt, or fear. These messages communicate in ways that say, "You should do this or you should not do that." Not everyone has a harsh "inner critic," but many of us do. Do you give yours the power to undercut you and make you doubt yourself? I have learned to listen to my "inner judge" and recognize it as the voice of my fear. It is usually communicating that I am not good enough in some way. I try to listen with compassion, knowing that it is a side of me that still is not healed.

PRACTICAL WISDOM

Genuine inner guidance directs you in a loving and compassionate way. This communication makes you feel open, warm, expansive, reassured, balanced, and full of peace. If you feel confused about the message and reach an impasse, become quiet, wait, pray, and meditate until you sense an answer that is both encouraging and loving. A true message from your inner guidance will be both practical and wise. Author Shakti Gawain explains it this way, "I've come to a point where I have a profound trust in my inner guidance. It's an unmistakable feeling of great love and power coming though me."

Everyone of you brings to this world your own unique gifts, talents, and abilities. You each have a piece of the puzzle that you are here to share with others. If you cast aside the inner guidance that continually informs you of your mission and purpose in life, you are not fully contributing your gifts. It is your uniqueness that makes you who you are. The puzzle will not be whole without the piece you have to offer. Your heart is a "truth meter" that indicates when you are heading in the right direction and if you are making the best decisions for your life path.

Your intuition provides the access to the divine plan that directs your life. Every experience that you have is helping you towards what you have

> **"WE ARE ALL PENCILS IN THE HAND OF A WRITING GOD, WHO IS SENDING LOVE LETTERS TO THE WORLD."**
>
> MOTHER TERESA

come here to learn. I am frequently asked, "Why am I going through this difficulty?" Understanding what purpose a particular challenge is fulfilling in our lives can be hard. Often the answer unfolds in time as the issue resolves.

Joanne, a student in one of my intuition classes, had a particularly unsupportive and difficult family. She asked her inner guide, "What is my life lesson?" She received the following answer in her meditation: "You have come here to learn to open your heart. You were born into a family that didn't know how to love and didn't give you much time or guidance. Your task was to learn to love these people despite their imperfections. As you have grown and matured, you have used the lessons of love and compassion and applied them to your counseling work with people who have mental illnesses. Your task in this life is to see beyond the imperfections and look to your soul for potential and love."

How can God be present for each of us, guiding our growth, life lessons, and purpose, and provide us with answers and comfort? I am not sure that is possible to know, considering the rational minds that we have in this human experience. But I have decided that it is okay that I cannot figure it out. Instead, I trust that a supreme intelligence created our world. This Intelligence provides us with higher understanding and direction via our innate inner guidance system. I trust that I will make the right decisions when I tap into my intuition. I know there is a force that operates powerfully within me and around me, and it shines its light on my being. If I trust it, I know I will not be led astray.

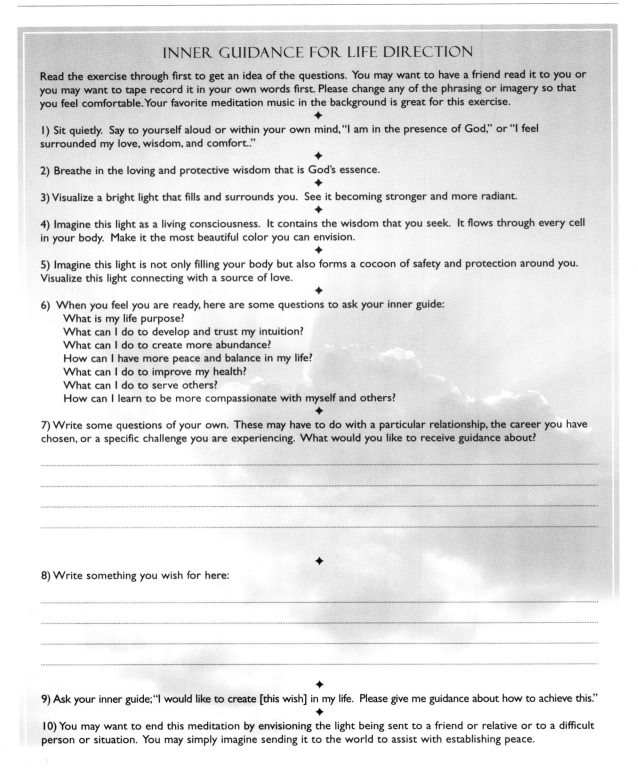

INNER GUIDANCE FOR LIFE DIRECTION

Read the exercise through first to get an idea of the questions. You may want to have a friend read it to you or you may want to tape record it in your own words first. Please change any of the phrasing or imagery so that you feel comfortable. Your favorite meditation music in the background is great for this exercise.

✦

1) Sit quietly. Say to yourself aloud or within your own mind, "I am in the presence of God," or "I feel surrounded my love, wisdom, and comfort.."

✦

2) Breathe in the loving and protective wisdom that is God's essence.

✦

3) Visualize a bright light that fills and surrounds you. See it becoming stronger and more radiant.

✦

4) Imagine this light as a living consciousness. It contains the wisdom that you seek. It flows through every cell in your body. Make it the most beautiful color you can envision.

✦

5) Imagine this light is not only filling your body but also forms a cocoon of safety and protection around you. Visualize this light connecting with a source of love.

✦

6) When you feel you are ready, here are some questions to ask your inner guide:
   What is my life purpose?
   What can I do to develop and trust my intuition?
   What can I do to create more abundance?
   How can I have more peace and balance in my life?
   What can I do to improve my health?
   What can I do to serve others?
   How can I learn to be more compassionate with myself and others?

✦

7) Write some questions of your own. These may have to do with a particular relationship, the career you have chosen, or a specific challenge you are experiencing. What would you like to receive guidance about?

8) Write something you wish for here:

✦

9) Ask your inner guide; "I would like to create [this wish] in my life. Please give me guidance about how to achieve this."

✦

10) You may want to end this meditation by envisioning the light being sent to a friend or relative or to a difficult person or situation. You may simply imagine sending it to the world to assist with establishing peace.

"MAN IS SO MADE THAT WHEN ANYTHING FIRES HIS SOUL, IMPOSSIBILITIES VANISH."

JEAN DE LA FONTAINE

INNOVATIVE SOLUTIONS

Author Marsha Sinetar writes that people who develop what she calls a "21st Century Mind" are "at home in the unknown; they listen to their inner voice and trust their intuition." They "envision creative possibilities and bring their own innovative solutions into the workplace, educational, religious institutions, and family life."

The philosophy and practice that you use when you tap into your "21st Century Mind" may be very different from other people's. But in a profound way you are not alone, as a greater consciousness in the universe is guiding us. What you call it or how you access it doesn't matter. When you communicate with this consciousness through your intuition it provides you with what you need to create your hopes and dreams. No two people travel the same path of awakening to their spirit. Life is always challenging you to develop new aspects of yourself. When you learn to tap into your inner wisdom and develop it, you can approach life in fresh ways.

Opposite is an exercise I call, "Inner Guidance for Life Direction." It suggests a way of connecting to God within you. You can begin this in any number of ways. Some people imagine a beautiful inner sanctuary that they go to in their minds in order to receive; others meditate or say a simple prayer. How you connect with and become aware of God's presence is up to you. Each of you has a sense of how best to proceed.

Intuition is often subtle. Your guidance rarely indicates that you make radical changes in your life without first suggesting gentle changes that leads you in the right direction. If you are going through a big transition in your life and are actively seeking guidance, create time for balance. Make time for meditation, prayer, retreats, walks in nature, or going to a religious service. Whatever appeals to you and allows you to find the answers of peace within are what you should move towards.

Remember that God speaks to you every day through your inner guidance. No great spiritual attainment must come first before you are found worthy of that wisdom. The voice of the Divine is as loud as our willingness to listen.

"WE ARE MEMBERS OF A VAST COSMIC ORCHESTRA, IN WHICH EACH LIVING INSTRUMENT IS ESSENTIAL TO THE COMPLEMENTARY AND HARMONIOUS PLAYING OF THE WHOLE."

J. ALLEN BOONE

"IT TAKES A LOT OF COURAGE TO RELEASE THE FAMILIAR AND SEEMINGLY SECURE, TO EMBRACE THE NEW. BUT THERE IS NO REAL SECURITY IN WHAT IS NO LONGER MEANINGFUL. THERE IS MORE SECURITY IN THE ADVENTUROUS AND EXCITING, FOR IN MOVEMENT THERE IS LIFE, AND IN CHANGE THERE IS POWER."

MARGARET STORTZ

WHEN INDECISION STRIKES

Most of us would just love it if God spoke to us in a clear, direct manner. "Hey Lynn! I know you're struggling with a decision in your life. Here's the answer..." Followed, of course, with detailed instructions about what I should and shouldn't do in order to be successful. In the Bible, God spoke to Moses from a burning bush. (I don't know about you, but if a burning bush started yelling at me I'd definitely run in the other direction!) But truthfully, don't you long for this clear kind of guidance when faced with indecision?

OUR MODERN CULTURE FOSTERS A GREAT DEAL OF IMPATIENCE. People want clear answers – and want them yesterday. In other times and other civilizations, more time was allowed for the process of change for a person to make difficult choices. People understood that there was a correct time for actions and decisions. If you look to nature you can easily see the rhythm of life, the ebbs and flows of the ocean, the seasons of the year when leaves die off and let go and when they are born anew in the spring.

Your life also has a rhythm and flow. Usually you experience an inner change or shift before the outer change begins to manifest. That is part of your inner guidance doing its work: you feel bored, restless, or anxious. . . things are not working as well as they once were. These are signs from your inner guidance that you must make some new decisions and new choices in your life.

The inquietude you are experiencing is telling you in effect, "Your present work is done. It's time for a change!" You can resist this impulse; you can say, "I don't want to change right now," or "It's inconvenient at this time." The feeling may temporarily recede, but that undercurrent of discontent will continue to nudge you until you take a conscious look at it and say, "Okay. Now is the time."

A client called recently to say that she was experiencing profound indecision about a job offer. Her company was merging with another, and she had been offered the CEO position of the new corporation that was being formed. She said, "Everyone is telling me I should take it. It's the obvious next step in my career. I know I have the skills to handle this job and, yet, I have no excitement about it whatsoever."

She was leaning towards accepting the new position because she had no idea about what else she would do. We talked for awhile about what she did find exciting and came up with a whole list of things that made her feel passion and enthusiasm. These interests did not point in the direction of a huge career change; they simply pointed out that her desires would not be served in the current job offer. Over the course of the conversation, the indecision she felt shifted from "I should take what's offered" to "I have some real interests and excitement about aspects of my work. My job now is to figure out what steps are needed to create a new work opportunity so I can do all these fun things and get paid for it!"

Author Richard Carlson says, "The trick to success sounds very simplistic because it is very simple: just begin. Take a single step, followed by another, and then another. Don't look too far out into the future, and don't look too far back either."

BEYOND THE COMFORT ZONE

Once you have recognized that you are ready for something new, you want it to happen immediately. You want the new job, new home, or new relationship to appear overnight. Sometimes it works that way. More often than not you have a little "work" to do in the process. You have to decide what you want, believe there is guidance available to help you create it, and begin to take the small steps on the path to your new dream. No doubt about it, it takes more than a small amount of courage to move in this new direction. I believe that God gives you hopes and dreams in a size too large so that you have something to grow into!

> "SAYING YES AND NO CLEARLY BUILDS CONFIDENCE AND RIDS US OF THE MISCONCEPTION THAT WE ARE POWERLESS."
>
> MARSHA SINETAR

> ❝YOU WILL DECIDE ON A MATTER, AND IT WILL BE ESTABLISHED FOR YOU, AND LIGHT WILL SHINE ON YOUR WAYS.❞
>
> JOB 22:28

You may feel uncomfortable while going through this transition. Understand that this happens to all people when they move out of the comfort zones of the familiar and known. You know the old adage, "The devil you know is better than the one you don't know." That thought has kept more people stuck in a rut with their lives on hold than any other! Motivational speaker Anthony Robbins addresses this issue when he says, "Concentrate on where you want to go, not on what you fear."

Your intuition is a built-in guidance system that directs you toward what makes you happy. It brings out the best in you and helps you learn what you have come here to master. Sometimes we get stuck in procrastination and cannot seem to budge. That is because you first have to discover what makes you happy.

BREAKING FREE OF OLD BELIEFS

How can you trust this guidance you are receiving? One of the primary laments I hear in my intuition classes is, "I feel like I'm making this up!" My explanation is that the voice of your inner guide or intuition comes to you in much the same way as your imagination – in thoughts, images, fleeting impressions, and the like. The solution I have to offer is to take some preliminary steps towards the answers you receive. If over a period of time your life situation improves, relationships are happier, you feel more joyful, and doors to opportunities begin to open, you will know you are on the right path!

The indecision and conflict you experience is often the universe letting you know that you need to break free of beliefs that no longer serve your personal or spiritual development. When you choose not to make a change as the result of these inner promptings, your intuition turns the heat up. You begin to feel more uncomfortable.

Change is inevitable in our lives. You can recognize that it is time for a change and heed the call by moving gracefully into the next phase of your life. You can also dig in your heels and yell at God saying, "I'm staying just where I am, thank you very much!" If you have indeed outgrown a way of life or a certain pattern of belief, you can be sure your intuition will continue to give you messages that a shift is needed. There are critical times in your life when the easiest path is to understand that change is necessary. At that point you need to listen to your inner guidance to experience peace again.

Every major decision means you enter into a new

> ❝IF WE LISTENED TO OUR INTELLECT, WE'D NEVER HAVE A LOVE AFFAIR. WE'D NEVER HAVE A FRIENDSHIP. WE'D NEVER GO INTO BUSINESS, BECAUSE WE'D BE CYNICAL. WELL, THAT'S NONSENSE. YOU'VE GOT TO JUMP OFF CLIFFS ALL THE TIME AND BUILD YOUR WINGS ON THE WAY DOWN.❞
>
> RAY BRADBURY

CHOOSING THE RIGHT PATH

1) What is the decision you are trying to make? Describe it here:

_____

_____

_____

_____

✦

2) Describe choice #1:

_____

_____

_____

Describe choice #2:

_____

_____

_____

✦

3) Sit in a quiet place, Create a relaxing environment. Light a candle and put on some quiet music. You might want to hold an object that has some spiritual meaning for you. This could be a cross, a rosary, prayer beads, a beautiful stone, or even a photograph of someone whose choices you respect and admire. Close your eyes. If you do not have a meditation practice, just watch your thoughts and notice your breath slowly flowing in and out.

✦

4) Bring choice #1 to mind. Pause. Then ask, where is this decision likely to lead?

✦

5) Bring choice #2 to mind. Pause. Then ask, where is this decision likely to lead?
(You can continue if there are more than 2 choices.)

✦

6) Pay attention to what you are feeling, experiencing, and sensing. This is your guidance directing you. Does one option have more energy than another? Which choice feels lighter or heavier? Do you hear an inner voice offering a compassionate message about your decision?

✦

If, after you have done this exercise work, you still have no clear call for action or strong feeling to do anything, it is usually better to wait. Sometimes waiting and being patient is all that is needed. You may feel compelled to take some smaller steps.

However, if you continue to find too many "closed doors" or you feel drained or overly anxious by the choice that you made, it is important to stop. See if you can find a place inside you that makes you feel peaceful or happy and try to follow where that feeling leads you. Above all else you want your choice to create more balance in your life, not more chaos and disruption.

"THE BIGGEST HUMAN TEMPTATION IS TO SETTLE FOR TOO LITTLE."

THOMAS MERTON

cycle of transformation, which may require new beliefs, a different spiritual path, a new career, the beginning or ending of a relationship. It may mean letting go of familiar people and places and moving on to another stage of life.

Do not let doubt and fear guide your life and your decisions. Accept uncertainty, anxiety, and even fear, as your companions on the path of change. You have made it this far in life. You are learning new skills, relying on your inner guidance, and making decisions that allow you to choose what makes you feel alive with excitement, not deadened with fear and frustration. Shakespeare put it this way, "Our doubts are traitors, and make us lose the good we oft might win, by fearing to attempt." Do you want to make your dreams come true, or your doubts? Have courage and be kind to yourself as you choose the path God is directing you to via your intuition.

Wonderful Things are in Store

When you decide to take action on your intuitive guidance you may attract a lot of resistance. Your friends and colleagues may think you're crazy for not taking that job promotion or for selling your house so you afford to pursue a new career path. You know that you are trusting your guidance and wonderful things are in store for you. Everyone else thinks you should have your head examined! In the movie *Oh, God!*, God (George Burns) commends the character played by John Denver and thanks him for bringing His message to the world. Denver responds, "You

know, everybody thinks I'm a nut." God replies after a short pause, "Galileo, Columbus, Thomas Edison... you're in good company!"

Melody Beattie writes in *The Language of Letting Go*, "When you wonder what is coming, tell yourself the best is coming, the very best life and love have to offer, the best God and His universe have to send. Then open your hands to receive it. It's yours." Your intuition will always be there gracing your steps through life. As you learn to access it and act on it is wisdom, you will find that your fear drops away and you will move forward with confidence in all your endeavors.

"BELIEVE IT IS POSSIBLE TO SOLVE YOUR PROBLEM. TREMENDOUS THINGS HAPPEN TO THE BELIEVER. SO BELIEVE THE ANSWER WILL COME. IT WILL."

NORMAN VINCENT PEALE

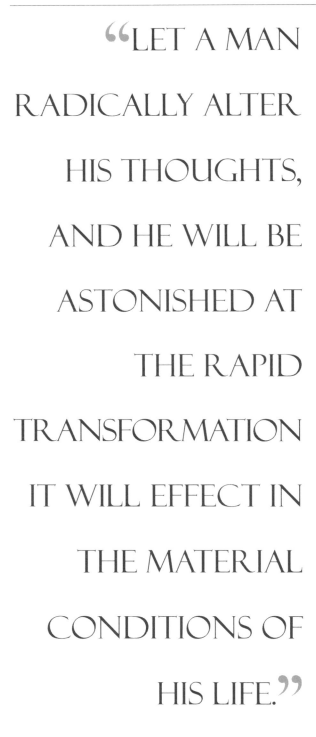

"LET A MAN RADICALLY ALTER HIS THOUGHTS, AND HE WILL BE ASTONISHED AT THE RAPID TRANSFORMATION IT WILL EFFECT IN THE MATERIAL CONDITIONS OF HIS LIFE."

JAMES ALLEN

CHOOSING "GOD THOUGHTS"

You know from reading the book this far that the power of your mind to imagine success is a key to creating a life you love. I practice watching and listening to my thoughts because I know that my attitude makes a difference in my life. "Thoughts held in mind produce after their kind," is a saying familiar to many Unity Church members.

HAVE YOU GOTTEN UP ON THE WRONG SIDE OF THE BED? Your day started off bad and got worse. Have you ever stopped yourself on one of those awful mornings and listened to what you were telling yourself? Here is what my thoughts sounded like on one of those mornings last week: "I can't write. I'll never finish this book. I might as well give it up. My friend Cheryl can write, but I can't. Nothing is working out. What if the publisher doesn't like my book? What if the editor rips it to shreds." You get the idea. (Grumble. Grumble. Grumble. Bah humbug.) That was *not* the beginning of a good day.

I have discovered that if I let myself go in this frame of mind for too long I might as well pack it in for the day. When I am in that state it is as if I am digging myself into a big pit. If I can break this pattern of thinking after a few minutes I can usually get myself out. If I continue shoveling the negative thoughts for a few hours, well, only a good night's sleep is going to get me out of that pit.

Thoughts are alive. They have energy. What you spend time thinking about becomes your habitual experience as you go about your life. The philosopher Soren Kierkegard wrote, "Our life always expresses the result of our dominant thoughts." If your thoughts are filled with doubt,

"A PARALYZED MAN WAS TELLING AN INTERVIEWER THAT HE HAD TRAINED TO BE A WORLD-CLASS ATHLETE BEFORE HIS ACCIDENT. THE INTERVIEWER ASKED HIM IF HIS HANDICAP HADN'T COLORED HIS LIFE. 'YES,' CAME THE QUICK ANSWER, 'BUT I'VE CHOSEN THE COLORS'."

GLORIA KARPINSKY

fear, anger, or any other negative emotion, that is what you are giving your attention to and thus what you are creating in your experience.

I practice watching and listening to my thoughts. I know that my attitude makes a big difference in my life. I try to turn my thinking around with "God thoughts." I am perfectly aware this sounds a bit simplistic. "What's a God thought?" you ask. A God thought is the most forgiving and loving attitude I can manage in my present situation, a way that I connect to my inner guidance in order to turn my attitude around.

IS THERE ANOTHER WAY?

Try this the next time you find yourself in the beginning of a bad mood. Take a few minutes to sit quietly. Take a deep breath and imagine you are filled with and surrounded by God's love. Bring to mind the issue that is upsetting you and ask simply, "Is there another way of viewing this situation that will make me feel better?" Open your heart and your mind and await the answer. Often the mere fact that you have asked the question will bring about the shift in consciousness that you need.

Each morning I wake up and I think about what I have ahead of me for the day. I imagine everything running smoothly and see myself achieving my goals, being calm, happy, and focused. I envision a healing light around me and around all the people and situations with whom I come in contact. I silently ask for inner guidance to be available to me throughout the day as I go about my tasks. I ask for help in remembering to tap into this wisdom whenever I feel confused, tired, or drained by something or someone. Your inner guidance is available in every moment throughout the day.

LIFE CHOICES

I realize I can choose to be in a good mood or I can choose to be in a bad one. Each time something negative or difficult happens, I can choose to be a victim or I can choose to learn from it. Life is all about choices. When you cut away everything else, each situation is a choice. You choose how you react

> "MUCH SO-CALLED 'POSITIVE THINKING' IS LITTLE MORE THAN WISHFUL THINKING, VOICING A LOT OF POLLYANNA WORDS THAT YOU REALLY DON'T BELIEVE. IT IS A MATTER OF SYNCHRONIZING YOUR SELF IN MIND WITH THE FLOW OF THE INFINITE. THE IDEAL, OF COURSE, IS TO THINK THE KIND OF THOUGHTS THAT LEAD TO THE KIND OF CONDITIONS THAT YOU WANT TO SEE MANIFEST IN YOUR LIFE."

ERIC BUTTERWORTH

to situations. You choose how people will affect your mood. When you find yourself slipping into a negative state of mind, learn to catch yourself and recognize you have a choice about how you perceive a person or a situation.

The Course in Miracles has a very simple, yet powerful statement: "I could choose peace instead of this." I often use this as an affirmative mantra to remind myself that the negative thoughts that are swirling through my head are my own creation. They are not God thoughts. In using this affirmation I silently ask God to help me change my thinking to thoughts that are more loving, hopeful, and absent of judgement. Use whatever prayer, mantra, or visualization that reconnects you with your inner self. Sometimes it takes just a moment of paying conscious

HOW CAN I FIND PEACE?

Try this the next time you find yourself in an upsetting circumstance:

◆

1) Sit quietly and focus on your breathing for a few moments or use any other technique that allows you to quiet your mind.

◆

2) Bring to mind the situation you find upsetting.

◆

3) Acknowledge to yourself that your goal is to experience peace and calm about this situation. Your task is to find a loving and compassionate approach to the resolution of the conflict you are experiencing.

◆

4) Imagine being filled and surrounded by a healing light or energy. Ask God to be present in whatever form feels right to you. Stay with this thought and image for a few moments.

◆

5) Ask the question, "How can I find peace in this situation?" Then rest quietly, trust, and listen. If your mind drifts to other things, simply repeat the question, "How can I find peace in this situation?" And listen again. Through prayerful listening, the answer will unfold.

◆

6) The next step is to ask, "Is there any action I need to take right now regarding this situation?" Listen and repeat, if necessary, as in step 5.

◆

7) Understand that you may not always receive an answer immediately. If you are feeling upset and unsettled by the situation you are praying about, your mind may not be calm enough for God's response to come through effectively. Trust that the answer will emerge over the next day. It may come in a dream, a shift in perception about your problem, a conversation with a friend, or something you are drawn to read. Or the answer may simply come fully formed.

"...WHATSOEVER THINGS ARE TRUE... HONEST... JUST... PURE... LOVELY... THINK ON THESE THINGS."

PHILIPPIANS 4:8

attention and then I can begin to focus on how I want to feel and what I want to create in my life.

Mary Manin Morrissey reminds us to "Set a positive intention for a 'God thought.' When you're stuck in a traffic jam, when the children bicker, or your partner seems uncaring, what happens to your

"WE ARE CO-CREATORS WITH GOD, NOT PUPPETS ON A STRING WAITING FOR SOMETHING TO HAPPEN."

FATHER LEO BOOTH

thoughts? In times of frustration and discouragement, our thoughts may sometimes turn to self-pity. Stick to your intention by remembering God in your thinking. Remember, nobody can rob you of a wonderful life without your consent."

Crises and catastrophes will continue to occur. Your relationship with God is a resource that can help you survive misfortune. Out of the suffering you experience, what choices do you make? Every difficulty you face presents you with an opportunity to decide how to respond. Your source of guidance, through your intuition, can help you become aware of more choices and resources for healing.

I believe that God's plan is for us to continue to choose love, forgiveness, and compassion in any and all situations we face. When you learn to consciously choose to take your mind off fear, victimization, and condemnation and put it on love, hope, and optimism, you are at the start of an extraordinary transformation. You are here to learn to love and be loved, and many of your lessons in life will assist you in making the right choices.

When you are faced with a situation that feels overwhelming, you can easily be consumed with thoughts of hopelessness and desperation. You do not know what to do. You cannot imagine feeling good again. You do not see a way to feel in control and you feel depressed and paralyzed. At times like these, remember that your inner guidance is connected to a greater source of wisdom. Your connection to God through intuition can provide you with new ways of thinking, resources to help you, and inspiration to direct you. Prayer is the way to speak with God. Ask for a transformation of your thoughts and feelings and you will be surprised at all the opportunities that open up before you.

THE PRESENCE OF GOD

Wayne Dyer offers this way of approaching prayer: "I center myself and empty my mind and begin to feel the love that is there when I quiet down enough to feel. As I do this I transcend time and space, and I am in the very presence of God." The next time you are searching for a way to resolve a painful situation try his approach: reach for a "God thought" whenever you are facing tough times. You will begin to do it automatically in everyday situations, and you will be on the path to discover a more peaceful, abundant, and contented life.

"THE SAME LIFE-FORCE THAT GROWS AN OAK FROM AN ACORN, A MOUNTAIN FROM THE EARTH'S MOLTEN CORE, A STREAM FROM THE SPRING THAW, A CHILD FROM AN EGG AND A SPERM, AN IDEA FROM THE MIND OF A HUMAN BEING, IS PRESENT IN ALL THINGS, ALL THOUGHTS AND ALL EXPERIENCES. THERE IS NO PLACE WHERE GOD IS NOT."

JOAN BORYSENKO

DIVINE GUIDANCE IN EVERYDAY LIFE

I have heard many clients speak of wanting "to be spiritual again." The comment always surprises me because I think our true task is to find and allow spirituality into our daily lives. You do not become "unspiritual" overnight. You do not wake up one morning and declare, "Oops! I've fallen off my spiritual path and I can't get up!"

RATHER, OVER TIME YOU PROBABLY MADE A SERIES OF SMALL CHOICES that have moved you away from God. You have forgotten to listen to the nudges and whispers of divine intuition.

You know what being spiritually disconnected feels like because you wake up irritated, you have a growing sense of unrest, your thoughts focus all too easily on everything that is not working in your life. The symptoms are many. Author Hugh Prather writes, "The secret to finding God is to understand that there is no great spiritual attainment that must come first. Anyone who wants to feel God's presence will feel God's presence."

YOUR SPRITUAL PATH

We often attribute spiritual consciousness to people who are religious leaders: cloistered nuns and monks, ministers, priests, and rabbis. But they are human beings, just like us. They have simply chosen their own path to spiritual enlightenment, and their choice of work reflects that. What about the rest of us who are mothers and fathers, clerical workers, hair stylists, businesspeople, teachers, and the like?

"THEY ONLY ASK, 'WHAT IS WRONG?'
SO ASKING THE QUESTION,
'WHAT IS RIGHT?
WHAT IS NOT WRONG?'
IS A GOOD BEGINNING.
BY ASKING IN THIS WAY
AND PAYING ATTENTION
TO THESE FRESH ELEMENTS
THAT ARE HEALING AND REFRESHING,
WE ARE ABLE TO HEAL OURSELVES,
TO GROW, AND TO GENERATE
JOY AND HAPPINESS."

THICH NHAT HANH

What does spirituality mean? For many of us it means a religion, going to church or temple each week. For others it may conjure up the notion of God sitting on a throne in the clouds as we await judgement. I choose to think of spirituality as a partnership with a universal wisdom that I call God. A grand design, a larger purpose to this life, resides in this wisdom that I feel flowing through me and all around me. I trust this wisdom enough to let it lead me. This guidance informs me through my intuition and shows me the path to find my true home.

I recently saw a bumper sticker that said, "Not feeling close to God? Who moved?" So, how do you get back on track if you're feeling unspiritual or disconnected? I find that writing in my journal is a wonderful way to remind myself what is important in my life. As I write, I ask in the deepest silence of my being for wisdom to come.

In this section are some questions to ask yourself to help you get back on your spiritual path. The thoughts and feelings that come to you as you write your answers are one of the ways God speaks with you. When you write the answers to the following questions you may feel an inner knowing bubbling up from within you. It may come to you in images or a feeling, or sometimes words may just pop into your head. However you receive it, write it down.

GUIDANCE IS ALWAYS AVAILABLE

You receive guidance in dreams, nudges, feelings, and sudden flashes of insight. Keep a notepad with you. Jot down any of your inner promptings that come as whispers from your soul. Pay attention to any directions you get that make you feel excited, exhilarated, or joyful. Also continue to write down any steps you can take to honor this guidance. Trust that God provides resources to help you follow your guidance. Your intuition is your pathfinder. When you learn to trust its inner prompting it leads you away from your indecision. It unerringly guides you on the right path to your happiness and fulfillment.

You may have heard of the movement that is known by the initials "WWJD." It stands for

"What Would Jesus Do?" There is another group promoting, "WWBD," which means "What Would Buddha Do?" There are probably as many of these associations as there are spiritual leaders. No matter what your specific religious beliefs or persuasion, decide that a source of wisdom is present in your everyday life to guide you.

JUST ASK!

Begin each morning by asking God within: "What would You have me do today?" Your guidance may encourage you to call a friend in need, resolve a dispute, begin working towards your hopes and dreams, forgive an enemy, or heal a hurt you may have caused. When you ask for and receive God's guidance you can bring a different response to the

DISCOVERING YOUR SPIRITUALITY

1) How do I define "spirituality"?

2) How do I know when I am following my intuition?

3) What do I think is my purpose in this life?

4) What are my unique gifts, abilities, and skills?

5) What makes me happy and fills me with enthusiasm?

6) What have I accomplished that I feel good about?

7) What do I like about myself?

8) What is working in my life?

9) What is not working?

10) I would love to...

11) I wish...

12) My intuition keeps telling me to...

13) When I have ignored my intuition in the past, I...

14) What steps should I take to bring God's guidance into my life?

> **"WHEN I STAND**
>
> **BEFORE GOD**
>
> **AT THE END OF MY LIFE,**
>
> **I WOULD HOPE THAT**
>
> **I WOULD NOT HAVE**
>
> **A SINGLE BIT OF TALENT LEFT,**
>
> **AND COULD SAY,**
>
> **'I USED EVERYTHING**
>
> **YOU GAVE ME.'"**

ERMA BOMBECK

challenges you face. You will find that the simple act of checking in daily with your inner guidance works miracles of healing in your life.

One of the ways you develop any skill or ability is to practice. You would not expect to be a concert pianist the first time you sat down to play the piano, would you? You'd probably laugh at anyone who

expected to be ready for the Olympics the first time they practiced a sport. Yet many expect to receive crystal clear wisdom after years of neglecting their inner guidance.

Developing your ability to hear God's messages requires practice. One of the main ways is simply to ask for guidance as you go about your day. When you begin checking in with your intuition on a regular basis you find answers to questions such as, "How should I handle this situation?" "Should I take this action or that action?" "Is this the best time for me to move ahead on this project?" "How can I be of help to my son in this situation?" By continuing to ask for guidance you are exercising your "intuition muscle." As you practice, you receive quick and ready insight to your questions, which leads you steadily in the direction of your hopes and dreams.

Sam Keen writes, "Nothing shapes our journeys through life so much as the questions we ask." When you are seeking divine guidance the quality of your questions determines the quality of your answers. Suppose you have a question about your career and you framed it, "What job should I take to make the most money?" Compare that to "How can I serve others by doing what I love and attract an abundance of money?" Another example is, "Why am I always getting sick?" Compare that to "What could I do to become strong and healthy again?" Let's try one more: "What's wrong with me?" compared to "What are some steps I could take to be happier?" Do you see the difference in intention in the rephrased questions?

> **"HIDE NOT YOUR TALENTS.**
> **THEY FOR USE WERE MADE.**
> **WHAT'S A SUNDIAL IN THE SHADE?"**

BEN FRANKLIN

"FOR I KNOW THE PLANS I HAVE FOR YOU. PLANS TO PROSPER YOU, GIVE YOU A FUTURE AND A HOPE."

JEREMIAH 29:11

In your ideal state you are kind, compassionate, and loving, and you use your skills and abilities to be of service in the world. When you are happy, fulfilled, and passionate about life, you are living your purpose. You find power in asking God for help when you are off track: "Is there a different way of perceiving this situation?" When you ask your inner guidance this question, you are asking the Universe to show you a more loving and wiser way of looking at things. You are aligning yourself with God, to keep you on track and on your path.

THE UNIVERSE IS ON YOUR SIDE

I am often asked about how to tell the difference between intuition and messages from your ego or intellect. The question is sometimes phrased, "How can I tell the difference between my fears or even wishful thinking and my intuition?" Messages from your inner wisdom are usually reassuring, loving, and contain guidance that makes you feel calm, peaceful, and confident. Messages from your intellect are often based on thoughts of lack, anger, guilt, or a need to protect yourself. If you are uncertain, find a quiet place inside yourself, listen, pray, and wait until you sense an answer that is reassuring and loving. The saying goes that when you pray, you do not change God but that God changes you.

I love this prayer that Benjamin Franklin prayed every day. Its language is old-fashioned but contains a potent message:

O Powerful Goodness, Bountiful Father, Merciful Guide, increase in me that wisdom which discovers my truest interest. Strengthen my resolution to perform that which wisdom dictates. Father of Light and Life, Thou Good Supreme, teach me what is good. Teach me Thyself. Save me from folly, vanity, vice, from every low pursuit. Fill my soul with knowledge, conscious peace, virtue pure, sacred, substantial, never-fading perseverance.

When you really start listening to and acting on your intuition instead of clinging to your old life, you will find yourself moving to the fulfillment of your dreams. The Universe is on your side. What fills you with joy is what is right for you. Richard Bach writes, "In the path of your happiness shall you find the learning for which you have chosen this lifetime." Continue to look within to the center of your being and know that the guidance you hear will direct you to your life's true purpose and meaning.

"I LEARNED THIS, AT LEAST, BY MY EXPERIMENT: THAT IF ONE ADVANCES CONFIDENTLY IN THE DIRECTION OF HIS DREAMS AND ENDEAVORS TO LIVE THE LIFE WHICH HE HAS IMAGINED, HE WILL MEET WITH A SUCCESS UNEXPECTED IN COMMON HOURS."

HENRY DAVID THOREAU

WHERE DO YOU GO FROM HERE?

When you listen to the whispers of your soul and take small steps forward, a new dream emerges. You have access to the gift of divine intuition to guide you to the fulfillment of that dream. Each time you ask for guidance and act on the wisdom you receive, you align your mind with the mind of God; you tap into a stream of conscious guidance that is divine intuition.

YOU GET A LIMITED NUMBER OF DAYS AND YEARS (AT LEAST IN THIS LIFETIME) and you do the best you can. You make choices and make the most of what you have in this life. The challenge for you is to live to the very best of your abilities. My wish for you is that you discover the river of wisdom, love, compassion, and guidance that flows through you and around you, that you tap its rich depths for insight and direction every moment, and find the heart of the thing you are seeking.

Anne Frank writes, "Everyone has inside of him a piece of good news. The good news is that you don't know how great you can be! How much you can love! What you can accomplish! And what your potential is!" No matter what life has handed you thus far, you have the opportunity to find pleasure, joy, love, and a sense of purpose. Dance and laugh. Take some risks. Try new things. Understand that the disappointments and challenges that are bound to come your way are there to help and guide you to a fuller, richer life.

"THE FATAL MISTAKE IS WAITING FOR LIFE'S CIRCUMSTANCES TO BE RIGHT BEFORE WE BEGIN. SIMPLY BEGIN WITH YOUR HEART, LOOK DEEPLY INTO IT, AND TRUST WHAT YOU FEEL. PRACTICE KNOWING AND YOU WILL KNOW."

HUGH PRATHER

> "SOMEDAY, AFTER MASTERING THE WINDS, THE WAVES, THE TIDES AND GRAVITY, WE SHALL HARNESS FOR GOD THE ENERGIES OF LOVE, AND THEN, FOR THE SECOND TIME IN THE HISTORY OF THE WORLD, MAN WILL DISCOVER FIRE."

PIERRE TEILHARD DE CHARDIN

A Life You Love

Here are the key factors in creating a life you love:

1. Identify your dream Deep inside, you have a vision. Some call it a sense of purpose, a mission, a destiny, or the call of God. Whatever it is, you feel restless and dissatisfied until you clarify it and take steps to fulfill it. It is the piece of the puzzle you have come here to contribute. What are you passionate about? What do you spend your time daydreaming about? What is fun for you? These are all components of your dream.

Many of my clients dismiss their desires out of hand because they immediately begin thinking they are impossible to attain. I have a request for you: Begin to dream right now. Do not limit yourself by trying to figure out how you're going to create this dream. That will stop you dead in your tracks. Guru Bhagwan Shree Rajneesh once admonished his followers to "Be realistic. Plan for a miracle." Take his advice. Your life can be about making your dream come true.

2. Visualize your success Capture the essence of what you want as a picture or series of pictures in your mind's eye. Close your eyes and vividly imagine the dream you want to create. Who is with you in this image? What are you wearing? How do you feel? Notice all the colors, sights, and sounds that surround you. Fill your image with emotion. Are you excited? Passionate? Full of energy? Write about your dream in your journal.

3. Move in the direction of your dream Decide to do at least one thing every day that moves you closer to your goal. It does not need to be a big step. Ask yourself, "What do I feel excited about today that will help me achieve my goal?" That is your intuition encouraging and nudging you. It is providing you with information about next steps and creating a sure and steady path to the achievement of your dream. Thomas Carlyle says, "Our main business is not to see what lies dimly at a distance, but to do what lies clearly at hand." Trust yourself, have courage, have fun, and do what needs to be done each day.

> "WHAT THIS POWER IS, I CANNOT SAY. ALL I KNOW IS THAT IT EXISTS... AND IT BECOMES AVAILABLE ONLY WHEN YOU ARE IN THAT STATE OF MIND IN WHICH YOU KNOW EXACTLY WHAT YOU WANT... AND ARE FULLY DETERMINED NOT TO QUIT UNTIL YOU GET IT."

ALEXANDER GRAHAM BELL

4. Turn over your concerns Learning to ask for guidance through prayer is deceptively simple. When you do it consistently, the results are spectacular. It does not have to take a lot of time or preparation. Sometimes it is simply a matter of stating, "God, what should I do?" or "Clear guidance is coming to me now." Each time you do this and are willing to wait in silence for your answer, you are widening the channel for divine intuition to pour into your heart and mind. Life will become far easier and less stressful. The next time you are troubled about something, try an experiment: Instead of mulling the issue over and over in your mind, ask God, "What should I do?" Then sit quietly and still your thoughts. Create a receptive and open state of mind and allow the answer to form. When you do this, something miraculous begins to happen. You are flipping on the switch to receive universal wisdom. Through your question and meditation, praying and allowing, you are opening the channel for this wisdom to inform you of the best course of action.

5. Follow the guidance you receive I once heard someone state that "If you are still alive, God still has plans for you." When you begin to trust and take action on your inner guidance, you begin to live your dreams. You are in touch with your divinely specialized mission for being on the earth at this time. You find a state of flow begin to emerge in your daily experience. Your life has balance and peace rather than stress and effort.

"THE 'STILL, SMALL VOICE' OF GOD NEVER CALLS ON ME TO BE LIKE ANOTHER MAN. IT APPEALS TO ME TO RISE TO MY FULL STATURE AND FULFILL THE PROMISE THAT SLEEPS WITHIN MY BEING."

SAM KEEN

The Universe provides you with precisely what you need when you need it. The doors to opportunity opens at just the right time to help you fulfill your dreams. Await God's guidance, nurture it, listen for it, rely on it, and act on it.

6. Surrender and trust I think Woody Allen was probably in the throes of surrender-and-trust when he exclaimed, "If only God would give me some clear sign! Like making a large deposit in my name at a Swiss bank." When you have done all the work in the previous five steps, you can be sure that everything will unfold at the perfect time. This is the toughest part for most people. You need to be patient through this phase. You have done everything you can do and you simply need to be at peace. When you are clear about your goals and intentions, at peace with yourself, and trusting your guidance, magic happens. People appear to help you, doors open, your world becomes rich with possibilities. What you need to do to realize your dream becomes real.

7. Appreciate and enjoy the life you have
There are many paths that can lead you to fulfillment in life. There is no one right way for everyone. Anything that keeps you focused on love, compassion, joy, forgiveness, serving others, and receiving guidance is the right path for you.

Write in your journal, follow your dreams, dance, live with joy, listen to uplifting music, go to religious services, read spiritual books, play with abandon, practice yoga, meditate, sing, show gratefulness everyday, pamper yourself, take a walk or go hiking, pray, hang out with kids, do what you love, daydream, sleep, go on a retreat, smell the flowers, ask for guidance, talk to others who can guide you on your spiritual quest, choose with no regret, paint, love your friends and family, draw, ask questions, take small steps, and keep walking. You are doing fine. It will all work out.

NEW JOURNEYS AWAIT!

God's will for you is to live the life that resides in your heart — the one that is made from your hopes and dreams. I wish you the best in the new journeys that await you. May you clearly receive your divine intuition and create a joy-filled and abundant life — and you love it!

HOW TO CREATE A LIFE YOU LOVE

1. Identify your dream.
   ✦
2. Visualize your success.
   ✦
3. Move in the direction of your dream.
   ✦
4. Turn your concerns over to God.
   ✦
5. Follow the guidance you receive.
   ✦
6. Surrender and trust
   ✦
7. Appreciate and enjoy the life you have.

LIMERICK COUNTY LIBRARY

BOOKS & RESOURCES

ALLEN, JAMES As a Man Thinketh (Andrews McMeel Publishing, 1999)

BLOCH, DOUGLAS Words That Heal: Affirmations and Meditations for Daily Living (Pallas Communications, 1997)

BOLEN, JEAN SHINODA The Millionth Circle: How to Change Ourselves and the World: The Meaning and Maintenance of Women's Circles (Conari Press, 1999)

BOOTH, FATHER LEO The Wisdom of Letting Go (Scp Limited, 1999)

BORYSENKO, JOAN Woman's Journey to God: Finding the Feminine Path (Riverhead Books, 2000)

BUTTERWORTH, ERIC Spiritual Economics: The Principles and Process of True Prosperity (Unity, 1998)

CADDY, EILEEN Opening Doors Within (Findhorn Press, 1996)

CAMERON, JULIA Transitions: Prayers and Declarations for a Changing Life (Jeremy P. Tarcher, 1999)

CARLSON, RICHARD Don't Sweat the Small Stuff--And It's All small Stuff (Hyperion, 1997)

CHOQUETTE, SONIA Your Heart's Desire: Instructions for Creating a life You Really Want (Three Rivers Press, 1997)

CONNY, BETH MENDE Believe in Yourself (Peter Pauper Press, 1998)

DANIEL, ALMA Ask Your Angels (Ballantine Books, 1992)

DYER, WAYNE Real Magic: Creating Miracles In Everyday Life (HarperCollins, 1992)

EMERY, MARCIA The Intuitive Healer: Assessing Your Inner Physician (St. Martin's Press, 1999)

FOUNDATION FOR INNER PEACE A Course in Miracles (Viking Press, 1996)

FRANQUEMONT, SHARON You Already Know What to Do: 10 Invitations to the Intuitive Life (Jeremy P. Tarcher, 1999)

GAWAIN, SHAKTI Living in the Light: A Guide to Personal and Planetary Transformation (New World Library, 1998)

JACKSON BROWN, JR. H. The Complete Life's Little Instruction Book (Rutledge Hill Press, 1997)

JEFFERS, SUSAN Feel the Fear…and Beyond: Mastering the Techniques for Doing It Anyway (Random House, 1998)

KARPINSKY, GLORIA Where Two Worlds Touch: Spiritual Rites of Passage (Ballantine Books, 1990)

KEEN, SAM Learning to Fly: Trapeze-Reflections on Fear, Trust, and the Joy of Letting Go (Broadway Books, 1999)

MANIN MORRISSEY, MARY Building Your Field of Dreams (Bantam Books, 1997)

MCMEEKIN, GAIL The Twelve Secrets of Highly Creative Women: A Portable Mentor (Conari Press, 2000)

NAPARSTEK, BELLERUTH Your Sixth Sense: Activating Your Psychic Potential (HarperSanFrancisco, 1997)

PEALE, NORMAN VINCENT The Power of Positive Thinking (Ballantine Books, 1996)

PECK, M. SCOTT The Road Less Traveled: A New Psychology of Love, Traditional Values and Spiritual Growth (Simon & Schuster, 1998)

PEIRCE, PENNEY The Present Moment: A Daybook of Clarity and Intuition (Contemporary Books, 2000)

PRATHER, HUGH Spiritual Notes to Myself: Essential Wisdom for the 21st Century (Conari Press, 1998)

RICHARDSON, CHERYL Take Time for Your Life: A Personal Coach's Seven-Step Program for Creating the Life You Want (Broadway Books, 1999)

ROBINSON, LYNN A. The Complete Idiot's Guide to Being Psychic (Macmillan Publishing, 1999)

ROSANOFF, NANCY, The Complete Idiot's Guide to Making Money Through Intuition (Macmillan Publishing, 1999)

SCHULTZ, MONA LISA Awakening Intuition: Using Your Mind-Body Network for Insight and Healing (Harmony Books, 1998)

SIEGEL, BERNIE Prescriptions for Living: Inspirational Lessons for a Joyful, Loving Life (Harperperennial Library, 1999)

SINETAR, MARSHA Sometimes Enough Is Enough: Spiritual Comfort in a Material World (Cliff Street Book, 2000)

ST. JAMES, ELAINE Living the Simple Life: A Guide to Scaling Down & Enjoying More (Hyperion, 1998)

SWINDOLL, CHARLES The Mystery of God's Will: What Does He Want for Me? (Word Books, 1999)

THICH NHAT HANH The Heart of the Buddha's Teaching: Transforming Suffering Into Peace, Joy & Liberation (Broadway Books, 1999)

WIEDER, MARCIA Doing Less and Having More: Five Easy Steps for Achieving Your Dreams (Quill, 1999)

WILLIAMSON, MARIANNE Enchanted Love: The Mystical Power of Intimate Relationships (Simon & Schuster, 1999)

INTUITION AND SPIRITUALITY RESOURCES

INTUITION NETWORK STUDY GROUPS
c/o INREACHING
1502 Tenth Street
Berkeley, CA. 94710
(510) 526-5510
e-mail: Inreaching@aol.com

INTUITION MAGAZINE
275 Brannan Street
San Francisco, CA 94107
(415) 538-8171
http://www.intuitionmagazine.com

INTUITION NETWORK
369-B Third Street, #161
San Rafael, CA 94901
(415) 256-1137
http://www.intuition.org

NEW AGE JOURNAL
New Age Publishing
42 Pleasant St
Watertown MA 02472
(800) 782-7006
http://www.newage.com

UNITY SCHOOL OF CHRISTIANITY
1901 NW Blue Parkway
Unity Village, MO 64065-0001
(816) 524-3550
http://www.unityworldhq.org

UNITY MAGAZINE
1901 NW Blue Parkway
Unity Village, MO 64065-0001
800-669-0282
http://www.unityworldhq.org

SCIENCE OF MIND MAGAZINE
3251 West Sixth Street
Los Angeles, CA 90020-5096
(800) 247-6463
http://www.scienceofmind.com

WORKSHOPS

Lynn Robinson gives talks and leads seminars all over the United States and in many other countries. Her topics include developing intuition, increasing financial abundance through intuition, and on techniques for creating a life you love. She is known for her on-the-spot intuitive insights about audience members.

AUDIO TAPES

Lynn produces a series of guided imagery tapes. Titles include "Prosperity! The Intuitive Path to Creating Abundance," "Creating the Life You Want," and many others.

FREE E-MAIL INTUITION NEWSLETTER

You'll receive a monthly digest by e-mail packed with information you can use, such as: valuable tips on how to develop your intuition, book reviews on topics of interest to readers, plus intuition and spirituality related web links.

INTUITION STORIES WANTED

Lynn would love to hear your intuition stories! If you have an inspiring or thought-provoking true story about how you've developed and used your own inner wisdom, please write or email Lynn at:

INTUITIVE CONSULTING & COMMUNICATION (IC&C)
P.O. Box 81218 Wellesley Hills, MA 02481, USA
800/925-4002 or 617/964-0075
E-mail: Lynn@LynnRobinson.com
http://www.LynnRobinson.com

ACKNOWLEDGMENTS

AUTHOR

A good book is a product of collaboration, so I consider myself fortunate to have had a wealth of support in creating *Divine Intuition*. Much gratitude and appreciation to: LaVonne Carlson for believing in my book and introducing me to Dorling Kindersley. My wonderful agent, John Willig, who is always ready with a sympathetic ear, helpful encouragement and a great sense of humor. Barbara Minton, my editor, who has been so patient and easy to work with. The designers, editors, and publicists at DK who have worked hard behind the scenes to make this book a success.

My dear friend and soul sister, Laura Walker, for her encouragement, support and most of all her friendship. Laura, it's so much fun to dream big dreams with you. Shane Brodock, my virtual assistant extraordinaire, who keeps me sane, focused, organized, and makes me laugh. You are such a Godsend!

My terrific friends, Bob and Gail Beck, Savita and Michael Brewer, Michael Gerrish, Shiri Hughes, Gail McMeekin, Marina Petro, Jean Redpath, Cheryl Richardson, Gayle Rosen, Barbara Selwyn, Mark and Beth Sullivan, and so many others. Thank you for being there.

My step-son, Cliff. I wish you many blessings as you continue on your path to creating a life you love. My husband, Gary. I feel so blessed by your love and support (and great editing.) I am very lucky to be married to you.

PUBLISHER

Dorling Kindersley would like to thank Claire Legemah for the original design concept, Jason Arnold for editorial help, Angela Anderson and Marie Osborn for picture research, and Louise Waller for DTP assistance.

AGENCY PHOTOGRAPHS

The publisher would like to thank the following sources for their kind permission to reproduce the images in this book:

Robert Harding Picture Library: 44, 60, 102, 152; Adam Woolfitt 36; Dave Jacobs 64; Douglas Peebles 30; Jeremy Bright 10; Raj Kamal 84.

Science Photo Library: Oscar Burriel 14.

Tony Stone Images: Art Wolfe 96; Darrell Gulin 18; David Madison 134; Ian Shaw 24; Jeremy Walker 118; Kim Westerskov 50; Roine Magnusson 56; Schafer & Hill 68.

Telegraph Colour Library: 146; Andy Glass 40; Benelux Press 90; Greg Pease 128; J.T. Turner 80; Jonathan Scott 74; Kathy Collins 140; P. Gridley 13, 17, 23, 29, 35, 38, 43, 49, 54, 59, 63, 67, 73, 79, 83, 88, 94, 100, 106, 110, 117, 121, 126, 127, 132, 138, 144, 149, 157; Ulf Sjostedt 112.

Geoff Ward: 108, 122.

DK PICTURE LIBRARY

Brian Cosgrove 8